Letts

KS2 Success

Age 7-11

Science

Revision & Practice

Philippa Hulme

REVISION GUIDE

Variety of Life

Growing and Changing

Your Body

Web of Life

Earth

States of Matter

Mixing and Making

Light

Space

Forces

Sound

Electricity

WORKBOOK

Why classify?

There is a huge variety of living things. Scientists **classify** them into groups so they can find out more about them. The living things in each group have similar features.

For example:

This gecko is an animal.

This sunflower is a plant.

The three main groups

Every living thing is in one of three broad groups. The groups are:

- **animals**, which eat other living things
- **plants**, which make their own food
- **microorganisms**, which are tiny living things that you can only see with a microscope.

Animals

Scientists divide **animals** into two big groups. They are:

- **vertebrates**, which have bony skeletons, including backbones
- **invertebrates**, which do not have backbones.

Each of these groups is sub-divided into smaller groups.
The table shows the five groups of **vertebrates**.

Group	Characteristics	Example
amphibians	damp skin, lay eggs in water	
reptiles	dry, scaly skin	
fish	scaly skin, fins, breathe underwater	
birds	feathers, wings, lay eggs	
mammals	hairy, live young, feed their young milk	

The three main groups (continued)

There are several groups of **invertebrates**. These include:

- worms
- animals with shells, such as snails
- arthropods, including insects and spiders.

Plants

Scientists divide **plants** into two big groups. They are:

- **flowering plants**, including grasses
- **non-flowering plants**, such as mosses, ferns and conifer trees.

Parent tip!

When your child finds an invertebrate, encourage them to observe it closely and to count its legs and wings (if it has any!). Make sure they care for it and return it safely to where it was found, or to a similar place.

Working scientifically

Classification keys

Riana makes a **classification key** to identify five invertebrates. She shows Dan how to use the key to identify an animal he has found at school.

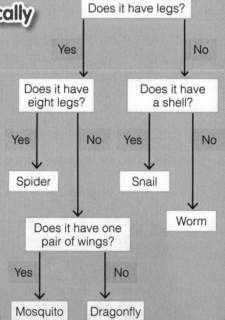

Classification key flowchart:

- Does it have legs?
  - Yes → Does it have eight legs?
    - Yes → Spider
    - No → Does it have one pair of wings?
      - Yes → Mosquito
      - No → Dragonfly
  - No → Does it have a shell?
    - Yes → Snail
    - No → Worm

Keywords

Classify ➤ To sort living things into groups depending on their similarities and differences

Vertebrate ➤ An animal with a bony skeleton and backbone

Invertebrate ➤ An animal without a backbone

Classification key ➤ A series of questions to help you identify a living thing

Have a go!

Go outside and find as many different types of invertebrate as possible.

- ➤ Classify them into groups depending on their number of legs, or whether they have a shell, or how many pairs of wings they have.
- ➤ Draw pictures of your invertebrates in their groups.

Test yourself

1. What do all plants have in common?
2. What is a vertebrate?
3. Name the five vertebrate groups.
4. Name two types of arthropod.
5. Look at the image and the classification key in the Working scientifically box. Use the key to identify Dan's animal.

What plants need

To live and grow, plants need:

- air, water and **nutrients**
- light and space.

Not all plants have the same needs.
For example, pineapples grow in warmer
places than apples. Pineapple plants grow
very slowly (and can even die) if it is
too cold.

Plant parts

Each part of a plant has its own job.

- The **roots** support the plant. They take in water and nutrients from the soil.
- The **stem** also supports the plant. It transports water and nutrients from the roots to the leaves and flowers.
- **Leaves** take in carbon dioxide from the air. When it is light they use carbon dioxide and water to make food for the plant.
- **Flowers** make seeds. See page 10 to find out more.

flower

stem

leaf

roots

Both the roots and stem transport water to the leaves and flowers.

Top tip!

Listen up 2

Working scientifically

Stem transport

Jamal wants to find out how water gets to a flower. He has two white flowers. He puts one white flower in a glass of normal water. He puts red food colouring in a second glass of water and adds the other white flower. Jamal writes his observations in a table.

white flower

red flower

water

red food colouring and water

Water colour	Observations
normal	The flower remains white.
red	The flower goes red.

Jamal uses his observations to make a prediction:

> If I put a white flower in blue water, the flower will go blue.

Jamal tests his prediction. He is correct. His teacher helps him to write a conclusion:

> Tubes in the stem carry water to the flower.

Keyword

Nutrient ➤ A substance that a plant or animal needs to survive, grow and stay healthy

Have a go! Put one stick of celery in normal water and another in a mixture of food colouring and water. Make careful observations and write them down.

Test yourself

❶ List five things that plants need.

❷ What is the job of a flower in a plant?

❸ Name two parts of a plant that support it.

❹ Describe two things that happen in leaves.

Growing and Changing

Metamorphosis

All living things change as they grow. Some change completely and the young look nothing like the adult. This is **metamorphosis**.

Frog

A frog is an amphibian. It starts life as an egg in a blob of jelly (frog spawn). It emerges as a tadpole, which gradually changes into a tiny frog.

Butterfly

A butterfly is an insect. It starts life as a tiny egg. A caterpillar (**larva**) comes out of the egg. It feeds and grows.

The caterpillar forms a chrysalis (**pupa**). Inside the chrysalis an adult butterfly is forming. Later, the butterfly emerges. If it is female it mates with a male butterfly and lays eggs. The cycle starts again.

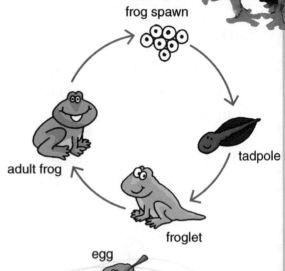

frog spawn

tadpole

froglet

adult frog

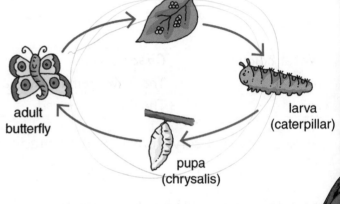

egg

larva (caterpillar)

pupa (chrysalis)

adult butterfly

Bird life cycle

A chicken is a bird. Like all birds, a female chicken lays eggs. If the female has mated with a male, a chick develops inside each egg. A few weeks later, the egg hatches. The chick that comes out grows into an adult chicken.

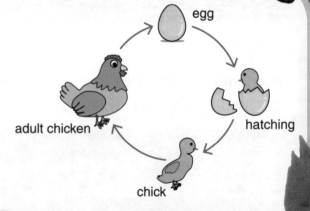

egg

hatching

chick

adult chicken

Top tip!

One way to remember the word **metamorphosis** is to think about something in a film or video game that changes into something completely different – by morphing.

Mammal life cycle

Humans are mammals.

You started life as a foetus inside your mum. You were born as a helpless **baby** and grew into a **toddler** and then a **child**. During **puberty** your body changes as you move towards **adulthood**.

The table shows some of the changes that take place during puberty.

Boys	Girls
body hair grows	body hair grows
penis gets bigger	breasts grow
shoulders widen	hips widen
voice deepens	periods start

Keywords

Metamorphosis ➤ When an animal changes completely as it grows

Larva ➤ The young of an animal that hatches from an egg. It is very different from the adult

Pupa ➤ The third stage in the life cycle of some insects

Puberty ➤ The stage of life when a child's body matures to become an adult

Listen up 3

Have a go! Search 'metamorphosis' on the Internet. List some animals that metamorphose as they grow. Make a file of photographs of animals at different stages of their life cycles.

Test yourself

❶ Explain what metamorphosis means.

❷ Name one insect and one amphibian that metamorphose.

❸ Put these stages for the life cycle of a frog in the correct order:

    froglet   frog
    tadpole   frog spawn

❹ List the four stages of the life cycle of a butterfly.

Life goes on

All living things produce young, or reproduce. Most animals, and many plants, reproduce by **sexual reproduction**.

New plants

Sexual reproduction in flowering plants involves making seeds.

1 Insects, or the wind, take pollen from the stamen of one flower to the stigma of another. This is **pollination**. Sometimes the pollen lands on the stigma of the same flower. This is self-pollination.

2 Pollen moves down to the ovary. Here, it joins with ovules to make seeds. This is **fertilisation**.

3 Seeds move away from the plant. The wind disperses some seeds. Other seeds are inside fruit. Animals eat the fruit. The seeds come out in their faeces (poo).

4 Seeds grow into new plants.

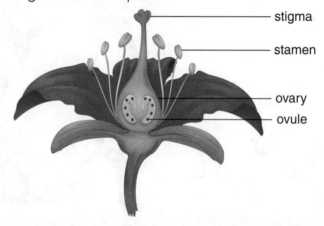

Some plants reproduce without seeds. This is **asexual reproduction**. It needs only one parent. The young are identical to their parents.

- **Strawberries** have runners. New plants grow from the runners.
- **Daffodils** make bulbs which develop into new plants.

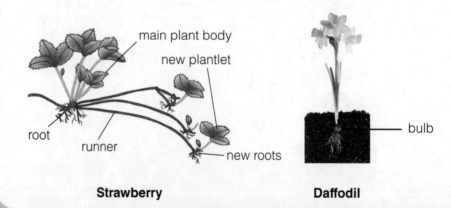

Strawberry　　　　　　**Daffodil**

New animals

Most animals, including humans, make their young by **sexual reproduction**. Sperm from the father joins with an egg from the mother. This is **fertilisation**.

In mammals, the fertilised egg forms a foetus inside the mother. The foetus develops and a baby animal is born.

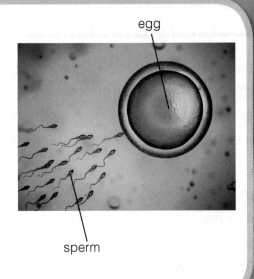

egg

sperm

Keywords

Sexual reproduction ➤ Making a new living thing by joining pollen with an ovule (in plants) or a sperm with an egg (in animals)

Pollination ➤ The transport of pollen from one flower to another

Fertilisation ➤ The joining of pollen with ovules to make seeds in plants, or the joining of a sperm with an egg in animals

Asexual reproduction ➤ Making a new plant without seeds

Parent tip! Ask your child to explain how flowers make seeds.

Have a go! Carefully use scissors or a knife to cut open a flower; for example, a lily, daffodil or fuchsia (ask an adult to help you). Can you find its stamens, stigma and ovaries? Afterwards, wash your hands carefully.

Test yourself

1. What is reproduction?
2. A blackberry plant is produced by asexual reproduction. How many parent plants does it have?
3. Describe one difference between pollination and fertilisation in plants.
4. Holly seeds are inside red berries. Describe how a bird would disperse holly seeds.

Circulatory system

All parts of your body need nutrients (from food) and oxygen. Your **circulatory system** takes nutrients and oxygen to where they are needed. It also carries waste away.

Your circulatory system includes your heart, blood vessels and blood.

- Your **heart** is a strong muscle. It pumps blood around your body. It beats about 70 times every minute.
- Your **blood** is mainly water. Nutrients dissolve in the water. Blood also includes red blood cells to carry oxygen.
- Blood travels through tubes called **blood vessels**.

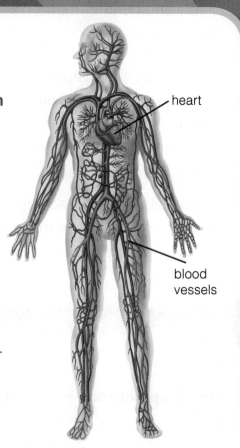

heart

blood vessels

Where blood enters and leaves the heart

blood leaves the heart

blood enters the heart

blood enters the heart

Blood vessels

There are different types of blood vessel, including arteries and veins. **Arteries** carry blood away from your heart to all other parts of your body. **Veins** return blood to the heart. The diagram of the circulatory system above shows arteries in red and veins in purple.

One artery joins your heart to your brain. It carries blood that is rich in oxygen and nutrients. Your brain removes the oxygen and nutrients that it needs. It replaces them with waste substances. The blood takes this waste away.

Listen up 5

Working scientifically

Measuring pulse rates

Your pulse measures how fast your heart is beating. Cora measures her pulse after resting, walking and jogging, by placing her fingers gently on her neck. She writes her results in a table.

Activity	Pulse rate after activity (beats per minute)
resting	80
walking	100
jogging	150

The results show that Cora's heart beats faster after exercise.

Keywords

Circulatory system ➤ The circulatory system includes the heart, blood vessels and blood. It transports nutrients and oxygen around the body

Heart ➤ The heart pumps blood around the body

Blood ➤ Blood is mainly water with dissolved nutrients. It also includes red blood cells

Blood vessels ➤ The tubes that blood flows through

Top tip! Remember, **a**rteries carry blood **away** from the heart.

Have a go! Sit still for a minute and then measure your pulse rate. Then run around for a minute and measure your pulse rate again. Is there any change? If so, can you explain what might cause this?

Test yourself

1 Name the three parts of the circulatory system.

2 What does your heart do?

3 Name two substances that are transported in the blood.

4 Look at the table in the Working scientifically box above. Predict what Cora's pulse rate might be after running fast.

Skeletons

Imagine having no bones. What would your body be like?

Humans have hard **skeletons** inside their bodies. So do all other mammals, as well as birds, fish, amphibians and reptiles. Your skeleton is made up of more than 200 bones.

Your skeleton has three main jobs.

- **It supports you** – it holds you upright.
- **It protects you** – e.g. your ribs protect your heart and lungs, and your skull protects your brain.
- **It helps you to move** – e.g. your skeleton bends at your knees and elbows, where bones meet and join.

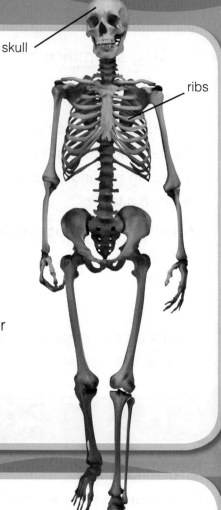

skull

ribs

Muscles

You have more than 350 **muscles** in your body, including your heart. Your muscles work with your skeleton to help you move.

Muscles are joined to bones. When a muscle **contracts**, it gets shorter and fatter. It pulls up the bone it is joined to. When the muscle **relaxes**, it goes back to its original shape.

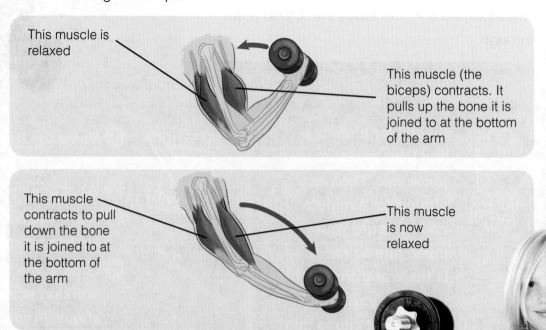

This muscle is relaxed

This muscle (the biceps) contracts. It pulls up the bone it is joined to at the bottom of the arm

This muscle contracts to pull down the bone it is joined to at the bottom of the arm

This muscle is now relaxed

Working scientifically

Comparing skeletons

Emma has two X-ray images. They show cat and snake bones. She compares the X-rays and writes down her observations.

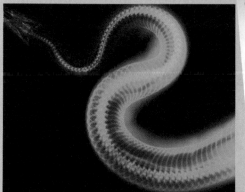

Both animals have a backbone and ribs.

The snake has more ribs.

Listen Up 6

Keywords

Skeleton ➤ The structure of bones in a body
Muscles ➤ Muscles help animals to move
Contract ➤ When a muscle contracts, it becomes short and fat
Relax ➤ When a muscle relaxes, it returns to its original shape

Parent tip!

Ask your child to tell you why their skeleton is important.

Have a go! Bend your arm, then straighten it. Can you feel your biceps contract and relax?

Test yourself

1. What is a skeleton?
2. A skeleton has three main jobs – what are they?
3. Name five animals that have skeletons inside their bodies.
4. Explain how your muscles help your arm to bend.

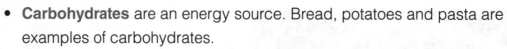

Balanced diet

Plants make their own food but animals cannot.
Animals, including humans, get their nutrients by eating.

There are different types of nutrients.

- **Carbohydrates** are an energy source. Bread, potatoes and pasta are examples of carbohydrates.
- **Fats** also provide energy. Butter, margarine and cooking oil provide fat.
- You need **proteins** for growth. They repair damage to your body. Meat, fish, milk and beans are full of protein.
- Fruit and vegetables provide **vitamins and minerals** to keep your body working properly. For example, vitamin D and calcium help make strong bones.

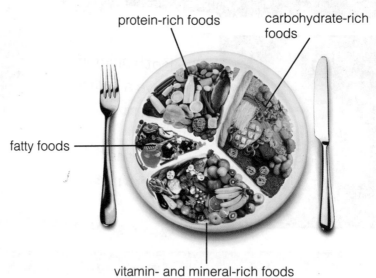

protein-rich foods

carbohydrate-rich foods

fatty foods

vitamin- and mineral-rich foods

To stay healthy you need all these nutrients in the correct amounts. Too much fatty food damages your heart. Too little vitamin D may cause rickets.

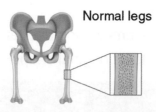 Normal legs

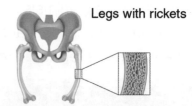 Legs with rickets

Listen up 7

Exercise

You need daily exercise for a healthy heart and strong muscles. Exercise can make you happy and help you to concentrate. If you do not exercise enough, or if you eat too much, you might get fat.

Drugs and smoking

Drugs affect how your body works. Some drugs are medicines. They cure illnesses or make you feel better. Other drugs, such as cannabis and ecstasy, damage your body and mind.

Alcohol is the drug in beer and wine. If you have too much, it damages many parts of the body, including the heart, stomach, brain and liver. Too much can kill.

Tobacco is the drug in cigarettes. It causes breathing problems, cancer and heart attacks. Over time, smoking kills people.

Keywords

Carbohydrates ➤ Nutrients that provide energy

Fats ➤ Nutrients that provide energy. Your body can store them

Proteins ➤ Nutrients needed for growth and repair

Vitamins and minerals ➤ Nutrients that keep your body working properly

Drugs ➤ Substances that affect how your body works

Parent tip!

Help your child to understand the differences between medicinal drugs and recreational drugs.

Have a go!

Read labels on food packets to find out which nutrients they contain. Are you surprised at what the labels say?

Test yourself

1. Name four different types of nutrients.
2. Name two foods that are high in fat.
3. Name four parts of the body that are damaged by alcohol.
4. Name two drugs that adults can buy at the shops but that can also kill.

Digestive system

Your body cannot use the food you eat just as it is.
Your **digestive system** breaks down food so that your body can absorb it.

1. In your **mouth**, your **tongue** detects tastes and your **teeth** chew food. Chemicals in your saliva start to break down the food.
2. Chewed food travels down the **oesophagus**.
3. In your **stomach**, chewed food mixes with digestive juices. The food starts to break down.
4. Partly digested food enters your **small intestine**. Extra digestive juices break down the food even more. Digested food passes through the intestine walls, into your blood.
5. Food that cannot be digested enters your **large intestine**. Here, water passes into your blood.
6. Your **rectum** holds undigested food as faeces (poo).
7. Faeces leave your body through your **anus**.

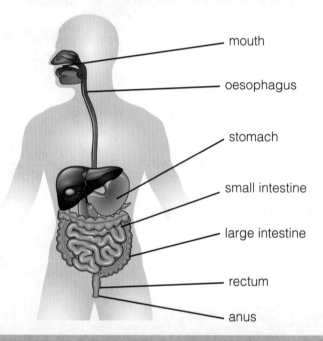

mouth

oesophagus

stomach

small intestine

large intestine

rectum

anus

Keywords

Digestive system ➤ Your digestive system breaks down food so that your body can use it

Oesophagus ➤ Chewed food passes down this tube from the mouth to the stomach

Stomach ➤ Digestive juices start to digest food here

Small intestine ➤ Digested food passes into the blood from here

Large intestine ➤ Water from undigested food passes into the body from here

Teeth

Teeth are an important part of the digestive system.
The three types of teeth are:

- **incisors**, which bite off pieces of food
- **canines**, which are pointed for tearing food
- **molars**, which grind and chew.

Humans have two sets of teeth:
20 milk teeth as a child, and later
32 permanent teeth.

It is important to look after your teeth by:

- avoiding sugary food and drinks
- brushing them twice a day
- going to the dentist for check-ups.

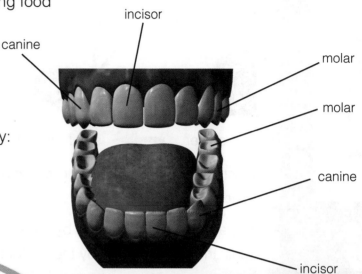

incisor

canine

molar

molar

canine

incisor

One way to remember the order of the parts of the digestive system is MOSSLRA: **m**outh, **o**esophagus, **s**tomach, **s**mall intestine, **l**arge intestine, **r**ectum, **a**nus.

Top tip!

Listen up
8

Have a go!

Use the Internet to find out how the teeth of a predator, such as a wolf, are different from the teeth of a grazing animal, such as a sheep. Can you explain these differences?

Test yourself

1 What is the job of the digestive system?

2 What happens in the stomach?

3 What are the three main ways of looking after your teeth?

4 Describe one difference in the appearance of incisors and molars. Give a reason for this difference.

What eats what?

Plants make their own food but animals do not. Instead, animals eat other living things.

Food chains show how animals get the nutrients they need.

Here is a food chain.

clover ➡ snail ➡ hedgehog ➡ badger

Most food chains start with green plants, such as clover. Green plants are **producers**.

The arrows mean 'is eaten by'. In this food chain the clover is eaten by the snail, the snail is eaten by the hedgehog and the hedgehog is eaten by the badger.

Animals that eat other animals are **predators**. Hedgehogs and badgers are predators.

The hedgehog is also a **prey** animal. It is eaten by other animals, for example the badger. The food chain shows that snails are the prey of hedgehogs.

Changes to one plant or animal in a food chain affect other parts of the chain. For example, if badgers are killed the number of hedgehogs might increase.

Keywords

Food chain ➤ A diagram that shows what eats what
Producer ➤ A living thing that makes its own food. Plants are producers
Predator ➤ An animal that eats other animals
Prey ➤ An animal that is eaten by other animals

Another snail food chain

Most animals belong to many food chains.
Here is another food chain that includes snails.

nettle ➡ snail ➡ frog ➡ heron

Parent tip! Reinforce the meanings of the words **producer**, **predator** and **prey** when you see plants and animals. Encourage your child to draw food chains that include the living things you see.

Use the Internet to find examples of food chains. What do you notice about how they are set out?

Test yourself

❶ **What is a producer?**

❷ **Look at the food chain above that includes a heron.**

   a **Name two prey animals in this food chain.**

   b **Which animal is both predator and prey?**

❸ **Draw a food chain involving a zebra, grass and a lion.**

What is an environment?

The **environment** of a plant or animal is the surroundings that it lives in. The environment provides everything that the plant or animal needs. It might also pose dangers.

Producer problem: a case study

Judy had grass in front of her house. Caterpillars and slugs lived in this environment.

The animals were part of many food chains. Here are some examples:

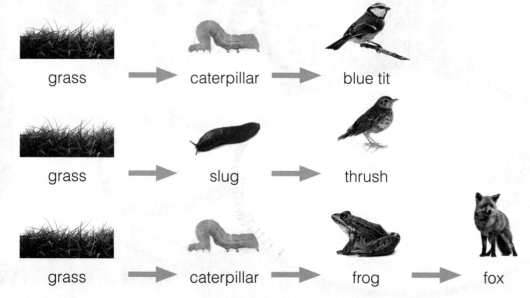

grass → caterpillar → blue tit

grass → slug → thrush

grass → caterpillar → frog → fox

Then Judy wanted somewhere to park her car. She dug up the lawn and paved it over.

The slugs and caterpillars had no grass to eat. Some of them died. Some moved away to find food elsewhere. The blue tits and thrushes had no slugs or caterpillars to eat. They died or moved away.

Removing the grass changed the environment. The environment no longer supplied what the animals needed.

Polar perils

Climate change makes arctic ice melt. This makes the environment less suitable for polar bears.

- There is less ice, so it is harder for polar bears to hunt and find prey animals such as seals.
- Distances between sea ice platforms are greater. Swimming between them is more dangerous.

Changes to the environment threaten the survival of polar bears.

Keyword

Environment ➤ The surroundings of a plant or animal. It supplies everything the plant or animal needs

Top tip! You can use food chains to help you predict what might happen if the environment changes.

Change for the better

Some environmental changes benefit living things, including nature reserves and garden ponds.

For example, the pond in the picture provides a perfect environment for newts.

Have a go! Use the Internet to find out how climate change has affected birds. Tell someone else what you have found out.

Test yourself

1. What does the word environment mean?
2. Look again at the case study on page 22. Predict what will happen to the number of foxes around Judy's house.
3. Explain why climate change is making the arctic environment less suitable for polar bears.

Adaptation

Every plant and animal has features that help it to survive in its environment. These features are **adaptations**.

For example:
- polar bears have a thick layer of fat to keep them warm
- meerkats have dark patches around their eyes to protect against the glare of the Sun.

Variation

The children in your class are not identical. They have different-coloured eyes and different-sized feet. The difference between individuals is called **variation**.

Living things produce **offspring** of the same kind as themselves. For example, cats give birth to cats and humans give birth to humans. However, offspring of the same parents show variation. They are not usually identical to each other or their parents.

Listen up 11

Keywords

Adaptations ➤ The features of an animal or plant that help it to survive in its environment
Variation ➤ The differences between animals or plants of the same type
Offspring ➤ The plants or animals that are produced by their parent or parents

Evolution

The animals and plants that lived many years ago are not the same as today. They have developed as a result of **evolution**.

This is how giraffes evolved.

1. The earliest giraffes had short necks.
2. By **natural variation**, some had slightly longer necks. They could eat leaves from higher branches. These giraffes were better adapted to their environment.
3. The better adapted longer-necked giraffes survived. The less well-adapted ones died. This is called the **survival of the fittest**.
4. The offspring of longer-necked giraffes were more likely to have longer necks.
5. Steps 2 to 4 happened again and again. Over many years, giraffes' necks became longer.

Charles Darwin played an important role in discovering and explaining evolution. He gathered evidence from detailed observations, many of which he made on a five-year voyage on a ship called *HMS Beagle*. He published his ideas in 1859, in a book called *On the Origin of Species*.

Top tip! Giraffes did not get their long necks by stretching!

Keyword

Evolution ➤ The development of plants or animals over many years

Have a go! Use the Internet to find out about the evolution of your favourite animal.

Test yourself

1. Describe how you show variation from your friends.
2. The eagle is a predator – it eats small mammals and birds. Describe how an eagle is adapted to catch its prey.
3. What does the word offspring mean?
4. Explain what evolution is.

Rock properties

There are many types of rock. Each has its own properties.

- Rocks can be **soft** or **hard**. It is easy to scratch a soft rock. It is difficult to scratch a hard rock.
- Rocks can be **porous** or **non-porous**. Water can soak into a porous rock, and some rocks are more porous than others. Water cannot soak into a non-porous rock.

Chalk is **soft** and **porous**:

Granite is **hard** and **non-porous**:

Crystals or grains?

Some types of rock are made up of **crystals**. There are no gaps between the crystals. These rocks are often **hard** and **non-porous**.

Some types of rock, such as chalk, are made up of **grains**. There are gaps between the grains. These rocks are **porous** and **soft**.

Keywords

Porous ➤ Water can soak into a porous material
Crystal ➤ A piece of solid material with a regular shape and flat faces
Grain ➤ A small piece of a solid material that does not have a regular shape

Listen up 12

Parent tip! Help your child to group rocks depending on their appearance or properties. For example, are they porous or non-porous? Are they hard or soft?

Fossils

Rocks that are made up of grains may contain **fossils**. A fossil is the remains, or traces, of a plant or animal that lived long ago. Remains include the bones, teeth or shells of animals, and wood from trees. Traces include animal footprints, or even faeces (poo!).

Here is how a fish fossil may form:
1. The fish dies and sinks quickly to the seabed.
2. Its soft body parts decay.
3. Layers of sand bury the hard body parts.
4. Over many years the hard parts form fossils.

Only a few individual animals or plants form fossils when they die. For example, most Tyrannosaurus rex dinosaurs did not form fossils, but a small number of them did. This is because many decay completely before they are buried, or are eaten. Some die in places where they could not be buried.

Fossils provide information about living things from long ago. They are evidence for evolution.

Soil

Soil is a mixture of **tiny pieces of rock, dead plants** and **dead animals**. It also includes **air** and **water**.

Different soils have different amounts of these things, and are suitable for different plants.

Keyword

Fossil ➤ The preserved remains or traces of an animal or plant that lived many years ago

Have a go! Outside, find as many different types of rock as you can. Look at them through a magnifying glass and draw what you see.

Test yourself
1. What is a fossil?
2. What is a porous rock?
3. Name the things that are mixed together in soil.
4. Do you think granite is made up of grains or crystals? Explain why.

The three states of matter

The different types of 'stuff' that things are made from are called **materials**. Materials can exist in different forms – as **solids**, **liquids** or **gases**. These are the **states of matter**.

One example of a material that can exist in different forms is water.

| solid water (ice) | liquid water | water as a gas |

The properties of a material depend on whether it is in its **solid**, **liquid** or **gas** state.

State	Shape	Can you hold it?	Can you squash it?	Does it flow and can you pour it?
solid	does not change unless you apply a force	yes	no	no
liquid	takes the shape of the bottom of the container it is in	not easily	no	yes
gas	fills up its whole container	no	yes	yes

Top tip!

It is not always easy to classify a material as a solid, liquid or gas. For example, you can pour sand from a bucket, but it is not a liquid or gas. You have to think about the separate grains of sand. Each individual grain is a small piece of solid.

Keywords

States of matter ➤ The three forms that matter exists in – solid, liquid and gas

Melting ➤ The change of state from solid to liquid

Freezing ➤ The change of state from liquid to solid

Conclusion ➤ What you have found out in an investigation

Listen up 13

Changing state

Imagine a piece of solid chocolate in your hand. It warms up and becomes liquid. This is **melting**. When liquid chocolate cools it becomes solid. This is **freezing**. Melting and freezing are **reversible changes**. It is easy to get back what you started with.

Different materials melt at different temperatures.

You can use a thermometer to measure melting temperatures.

Melting chocolate

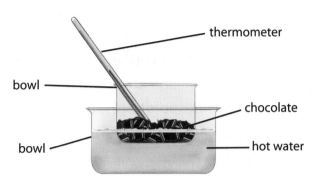

- thermometer
- bowl
- chocolate
- bowl
- hot water

Working scientifically

Melting temperatures

You can use results to make **conclusions**.

Sarah measures the melting temperatures of butter, chocolate and ice. She presents her results in a bar chart.

Sarah uses her results to write a conclusion:

> The butter and chocolate both melted at 37 °C. The ice melted at a lower temperature, at around 0 °C.

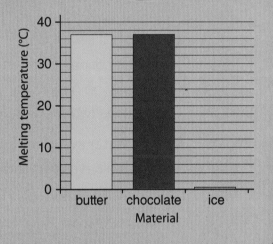

At home, find some materials in the solid, liquid and gas states. Write down their names and which states they are in.

Hint: You cannot see most gases but they are all around you. You can smell some gases.

Test yourself

❶ Name the three states of matter.

❷ Name the change of state when a material changes from solid to liquid.

❸ Describe two differences between a material in its solid and liquid states.

Evaporating and condensing

On a warm day, a puddle disappears. The liquid water has formed water vapour. **Water vapour** is water in the gas state. The change of state from liquid to gas is called **evaporating**. Most liquids evaporate when they are heated.

There is water vapour in the air. When water vapour hits a cold surface, like the inside of a window, it becomes liquid. The change from gas to liquid is called **condensing**. Most gases condense when they are cooled.

Evaporating and condensing are **reversible changes**.

Working scientifically

Speeding up evaporation

Ben notices that puddles disappear faster on hot or windy days. He makes two **predictions**:

> Water evaporates faster at higher temperatures.
>
> Water evaporates faster in moving air.

Ben does two experiments. He finds out that his predictions are correct:
- The higher the temperature, the faster water evaporates.
- The faster the air is moving, the faster water evaporates.

Keywords

Evaporate ➤ The change of state from liquid to gas

Condense ➤ The change of state from gas to liquid

Prediction ➤ What you expect to happen in an investigation, based on something you already know or have observed

Top tip!

Remember that e**vap**orating makes water **vap**our. Water vapour is water in the gas state.

Listen up 14

The water cycle

The **water cycle** describes the movement of water on Earth.

A number of processes are involved in the water cycle.

1. The Sun heats liquid water on land and in rivers, lakes and seas. Some evaporates, forming water vapour.

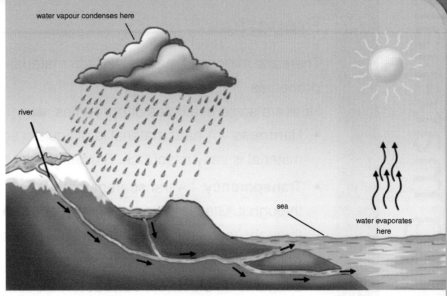

water vapour condenses here

river

sea

water evaporates here

2. Water vapour cools as it rises. It condenses into tiny droplets of liquid water. The droplets form clouds.
3. The clouds get heavy. Liquid water falls from them as rain.
4. Rain falls on land and sea. The rain that falls on land flows into streams and rivers, and returns to the sea.

Keyword

Water cycle ➤ The journey water takes as it circulates from rivers, lakes and seas to the sky and back again

Have a go!

Place a few drops of water on two pieces of kitchen roll. Put one piece in a warm place and one in a cool place. Where does the water evaporate faster?

Test yourself

1. Name the change of state from liquid to gas.
2. Name the change of state from gas to liquid.
3. The table gives the average temperature over one year for two cities.

City	Average temperature (°C)
Moscow, Russia	6
Dar es Salaam, Tanzania	26

Predict whether water will evaporate more quickly on a dry day in Moscow or on a dry day in Dar es Salaam.

4. Explain why evaporation is important in the water cycle.

Properties

There are millions of materials. Each material has its own properties.

Here are some examples of properties.

- **Hardness** – A hard material is difficult to scratch. A soft material is easy to scratch. Steel is harder than wood.

- **Transparency** – A transparent material lets light through. You can see through it. Glass is transparent. An **opaque** material does not allow light through. You cannot see through it. Wood is opaque.

- **Electrical conductivity** – Electricity travels easily through copper, so copper is an **electrical conductor**. Electricity cannot travel through wood, so wood is an **electrical insulator**.

- **Thermal conductivity** – Heat travels more easily through some materials than others. Heat travels easily through copper, so copper is a good **thermal conductor**. Heat does not travel easily through wood, so wood is a **thermal insulator**.

- **Response to magnets** – Magnets are attracted to iron and steel. Iron and steel are **magnetic**. Two other magnetic materials are nickel and cobalt.

Using materials

The properties of different materials make them useful for different jobs.

For example:

- glass is transparent – it makes good windows

- copper is a good electrical conductor – it is used in wires.

Working scientifically

Choosing an insulator

Ellie wants to find out if paper or fleece keeps soup warmer. She does a **fair test** to find out.

The amount of soup in each cup is the same. The paper and fleece are the same thickness. Ellie uses a thermometer to check that both cups of soup start off at the same temperature.

After 10 minutes, Ellie uses a thermometer to measure the temperature of the soup in cup A and cup B. The soup in cup B is warmer than the soup in cup A. This shows that fleece is a better thermal insulator than paper.

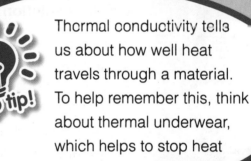

Thermal conductivity tells us about how well heat travels through a material. To help remember this, think about thermal underwear, which helps to stop heat leaving your body.

Keywords

Hardness ➤ How easy it is to scratch a material. A hard material is difficult to scratch

Transparency ➤ A substance is transparent if it lets light through

Conductivity ➤ How easy it is for electricity or heat to travel through a material. The higher the value for electrical conductivity of a material, the more easily electricity travels through it

Fair test ➤ An investigation where you keep all the variables the same except the ones that you are changing and measuring

Find an object in the kitchen. What material is it made from? How do the properties of the material make it suitable for its use? Repeat with two more objects.

❶ What is a transparent material?

❷ Write down four properties of wood.

❸ You can scratch steel with diamond. Which material is harder?

Separating by sieving

mixture of sand and stones · sieve · sand

Imagine that a child drops many small stones into his sandpit. This makes a **mixture** of sand and stones. How can he get the stones out without missing any?

Mixing is a **reversible change**, so it is easy to get back the original materials. **Sieving** separates pieces of solid of different sizes.

Dissolving and evaporating

Imagine adding salt to water, and stirring. Soon you cannot see the salt. However, the salt is still there. It is mixed up with the water. The salt has **dissolved** to make a **solution**.

Dissolving is a **reversible** change, so you can separate substances from a solution.

If you leave salt solution on a plate in a warm room, the water evaporates. The salt stays on the plate. The mixture has been separated by evaporation.

Day 1 · salt solution · Five days later · salt

Separating by filtering

Salt dissolves in water. It is **soluble**. However, some substances are not soluble. Sand never dissolves in water, no matter how much you stir it. Sand is not soluble.

You can use **sieving** or **filtering** to separate water from a substance that is not soluble (like sand).

filter paper · filter funnel · sand · water

Working scientifically

Soluble or not?

Sam wants to find out if some substances are soluble. He creates a table to record his data. He writes the **variable** he changes in the left-hand column (the substance), and the variable he observes (Does it dissolve?) in the other column.

Substance	Does it dissolve?
sugar	
flour	
cornflakes	

Keywords

Mixture ➤ A mixture is made up of two or more materials. It is often easy to separate the materials in a mixture

Reversible change ➤ A change in which you can get the original materials back. New substances are not made

Dissolving ➤ Mixing a solid with a liquid to make a solution

Solution ➤ A mixture of a solid with a liquid. You cannot see pieces of solid in a solution

Soluble ➤ A material is soluble if it dissolves in water

Variable ➤ Something you can change, measure or keep the same in an investigation

Listen up 16

Parent tip!

Help your child to understand that dissolving, mixing and changes of state are reversible. This means that it is usually easy to get the starting materials back.

Have a go!

Add one spoonful of sugar to a glass of water. Does it dissolve? Repeat with two other substances. Are they soluble? Record your data in a table, like the one in the Working scientifically box.

Test yourself

1. What is a mixture?
2. Give examples of three types of reversible change.
3. Name a technique for separating sugar from sugar solution.
4. Filter paper has tiny holes. Use this information to suggest how filtration separates sand from water.

Burning and rusting

Wood burns on a bonfire, forming ash, smoke and invisible gases. Burning is a change that is **not reversible**. Changes that are not reversible make new materials. You cannot get the starting materials back again.

This car is rusty. Its metal has joined with materials from the air to make a new material, rust. Rusting is not reversible.

Useful changes

Most changes that happen in cooking are difficult to reverse. For example:

- you cannot get back the sugar, eggs, flour and butter when you bake a cake.

The materials we use every day were made from changes that are difficult to reverse. For example:

- wood comes from trees (which use carbon dioxide and water to grow)
- polythene is made in factories from a gas that comes from oil.

Keyword

Not reversible ➤ A change that is not reversible makes new materials. It is difficult – or impossible – to get the starting materials back again

Working scientifically

Vinegar and bicarbonate of soda

Catherine and Sarah investigate a change that is difficult to reverse. They add a white powder, bicarbonate of soda, to vinegar. They see bubbles of a new material. The bubbling stops when the powder is used up.

The girls predict that the change will be quicker if the vinegar is warmer. They measure the time for the bubbling to stop at three different temperatures.

They make sure they do a fair test by **controlling** two **variables** – the amount of vinegar and the amount of powder.

Catherine and Sarah find out that their prediction is correct: the warmer the vinegar, the quicker the change.

Keyword

Control variables ➤ The variables you keep the same in a fair test

Parent tip!

Discuss examples of changes that are reversible and those that are not usually reversible. For example, burning a match is not usually reversible but melting ice is reversible.

Have a go!

Do this activity with an adult.

➤ Light a candle and observe carefully. Identify one reversible change.

➤ Can you see any materials that were made in a change that is not reversible?

Test yourself

❶ What is a control variable?

❷ Underline the two reversible changes:

    burning   melting

    rusting   dissolving

❸ Describe one difference between a reversible change and a change that is not reversible.

❹ Is making toast a reversible change or a change that is not reversible? Explain your decision.

Light sources

Some objects make light. These are **light sources**. Light sources include the Sun, other stars, lamps, torches, candles, computer screens and televisions.

You can see a light source when light travels from the source to your eye. Light travels in straight lines.

You must never look directly at the Sun. Its bright light can damage your eyes, even if you are wearing sunglasses.

Reflecting light

Most objects are not light sources. Their surfaces **reflect** light.

This is how you see a ball outside:

1 Light from the Sun (a light source) travels in a straight line to the ball.
2 The surface of the ball reflects light.
3 Reflected light from the ball travels in a straight line to your eye.

Shiny surfaces reflect more light than dull surfaces. Light-coloured surfaces reflect more light than dark ones. You cannot see anything when there is no light, in a completely dark room.

Keywords

Light source ➤ An object that makes light

Reflect ➤ Light is reflected when it bounces off a surface

Working scientifically

Perfect periscope

Elliot is 150 cm tall. He wants to see over adults' heads in a crowd.
Elliot decides to make a periscope. The diagram shows how it works.

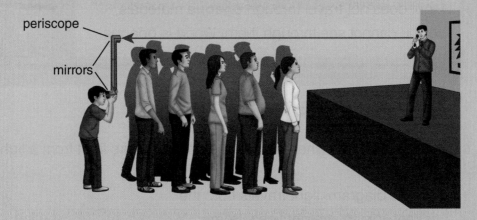

periscope

mirrors

Elliot needs to know how tall to make his periscope. He collects data by measuring the heights of five adults. He calculates their average height, which is 168 cm. He also writes down the height of the tallest person, which is 190 cm. Elliot uses this data, and his own height, to work out the best height for his periscope.

The Moon is not a light source. You can see it because it reflects light from the Sun.

Top tip!

Make a list of all the light sources you can find around your home.

Have a go!

Test yourself

1. Name five light sources.
2. Which reflects more candlelight – a mirror or a piece of black paper of the same size?
3. Draw a diagram to explain how you see a cuddly toy when you shine a torch at it.
4. Look again at the Working scientifically box. Use the data to calculate the best height for Elliot's periscope. Show how you worked out your answer.

Transparent or opaque?

Light travels through transparent materials. That is why you can see through glass, or parts of this butterfly's wing.

Light does not travel through **opaque** materials, so you cannot see through them. Wood is opaque.

Making shadows

A **shadow** forms when an opaque object blocks light from a light source.

In this diagram, light travels from the street light in straight lines. Some light hits the cat. This light travels no further. There is an area of darkness, or shadow, behind the cat.

Some light from the street light travels past the cat. This is why there is light around the shadow.

Lengthening shadows

The size of a shadow depends on the position of the light source.

At midday the Sun is above you in the sky. Your shadow is short. In the evening the Sun is low in the sky. Your shadow is longer.

Short shadow   **Long shadow**

Keywords

Opaque ➤ Light cannot travel through an opaque object

Shadow ➤ An area of darkness on a surface caused by an opaque object blocking out light

Listen up 19

Working scientifically

Shadow size

Joshua asks a scientific question:

> How does the angle of a light source affect the length of a shadow?

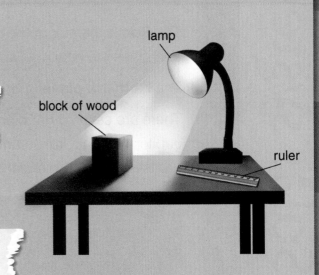

lamp

block of wood

ruler

Joshua plans an investigation to answer his question. He decides which variables to change, measure and control:

- variable to change – angle of light source
- variable to measure – length of shadow
- variables to control – size and shape of object

Joshua collects some data. He finds out that the smaller the angle of the light source above the table, the longer the shadow.

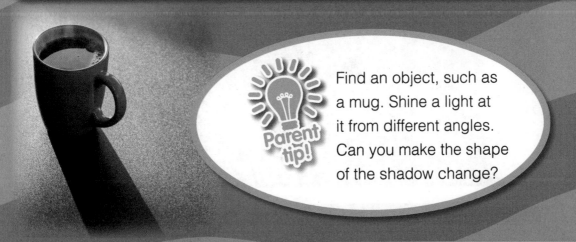

Parent tip!

Find an object, such as a mug. Shine a light at it from different angles. Can you make the shape of the shadow change?

Have a go!

Take a torch into a dark room. Use your hand and the torch to make shadows on the wall. Can you make them bigger and smaller?

Test yourself

1. What is a shadow?
2. What is the difference between a transparent object and an opaque object?
3. Look again at the Working scientifically box. Name one piece of equipment that Joshua needs for his investigation.
4. Constance has a shadow puppet. How can she make the shadow bigger?

The solar system

The **Sun** is the star at the centre of our **solar system**. It is a light source and gives out heat. It is spherical.

The Earth is a **planet** that orbits the Sun. Its shape is roughly spherical.

There are seven other planets in our solar system: Mercury, Venus, Mars, Jupiter, Saturn, Uranus and Neptune. All the planets **orbit** the Sun. Their orbits are roughly circular.

The Moon

A **moon** is a natural object that orbits a planet. Jupiter has four big moons and many more small ones.

The Earth has one moon. It is roughly spherical. The Moon takes 27 days to orbit Earth.

Working scientifically

Ideas about the solar system

Ptolemy was a scientist. He lived in Egypt, two thousand years ago. Ptolemy used observations from other scientists, and his own ideas, to develop a theory. The Earth is at the centre of the Universe, he said. The Sun, and other planets, orbit Earth.

One thousand years later, an Arab scientist, Alhazen, noticed some problems with Ptolemy's ideas. He wrote a book to explain these problems.

Copernicus (1473–1543)

Copernicus lived in Poland five hundred years ago. He also criticised Ptolemy's theory. He thought it unlikely that thousands of stars could orbit Earth every 24 hours. It is more likely that Earth is rotating, he said. Copernicus developed a new theory, that the Earth and other planets orbit the Sun.

Parent tip!

The section above on ideas about our solar system shows how scientific theories can change over time as new evidence is obtained.

Keywords

Sun ➤ The star at the centre of our solar system

Solar system ➤ The Sun, and the planets and other objects that orbit it

Planet ➤ A big object that orbits a star

Orbit ➤ The circular (or elliptical) path an object in space takes around another object in space

Moon ➤ A natural object that orbits a planet

Have a go!

Use the Internet to find out as much as you can about a planet of your choice. Make a poster to display your findings.

Test yourself

❶ What object does the Earth orbit?

❷ What object does the Moon orbit?

❸ Describe one way in which the Sun, Earth and Moon are similar.

❹ Describe one difference between the Earth and the Moon.

Day and night

The Earth is rotating on its **axis**. The Earth takes 24 hours to rotate once.

The rotating Earth gives us day and night. At any one time, half the Earth faces the Sun. This part of the Earth is light, so it is daytime here. The other half of the Earth faces away from the Sun. This part of the Earth is in darkness. It is night-time here.

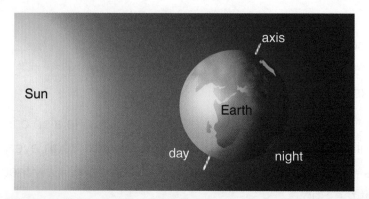

From east to west

The Sun **appears to move** across the sky, from east to west. In fact, it is the Earth that is moving; the Sun is stationary.

The Earth rotates towards the east. This explains why we see the Sun rise in the east in the morning. As the Earth continues to spin, the Sun appears to move across the sky. In the evening the Sun sets in the west.

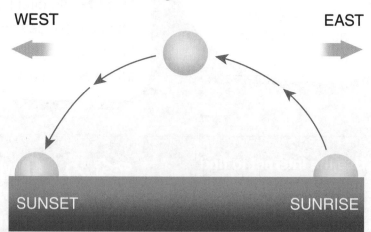

Keyword

Axis ➤ An imaginary line between the North Pole and the South Pole, going through the centre of the Earth

Working scientifically

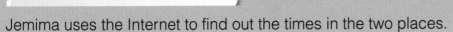

Peru

Time of day

One day after school, Jemima looks at her globe. She notices that Peru and Singapore are on opposite sides of the Earth.

She makes a prediction:

> When it is daytime in Peru, it is night-time in Singapore.

Jemima uses the Internet to find out the times in the two places.

Place	Time
Peru	11:00 (morning)
Singapore	23:00 (night)

The data show that her prediction is correct.

Don't confuse the scientific meaning of the word **day** (the time for the Earth to rotate once on its axis) with the usual meaning of the word **day** (daytime, the part of the day when it is light).

Top tip!

Use a ball and a torch to model the Earth rotating on its axis. Can you use your model to explain why we have day and night?

Have a go!

Test yourself

❶ How long does the Earth take to rotate on its axis?

❷ In which direction does the Earth rotate – towards the east or west?

❸ Explain why it is sometimes dark and sometimes light.

❹ Explain why the Sun seems to move across the sky.

What can forces do?

Forces can be pushes or pulls. They can make things move, and make them move faster. They can slow things down and make them stop.

Forces also change the direction of moving objects. They change shapes too, by squashing and stretching.

Friction

Friction is a force that acts against things that are moving.

For example, to make a bike start moving, you must overcome the friction between the tyre and the road. When you pull on the brakes, the force of friction between the brake blocks and the tyres makes the bike stop.

Air resistance and water resistance

Air resistance and water resistance make things slow down.

When you swim, you experience **water resistance**.

Flying birds and falling parachutes experience **air resistance**.

Listen up
22

Keywords

Forces ➤ Forces can change the movement and shapes of objects

Friction ➤ A force that acts between surfaces and slows down or stops things that are moving

Water resistance ➤ A force that slows things down in water

Air resistance ➤ A force that slows things down in air

Working scientifically

Surfaces and friction

Callum asks a scientific question:

> Is there more friction between rough surfaces or smooth ones?

Check that your child knows that friction, air resistance and water resistance are **contact forces**. They act between moving surfaces.

Parent tip!

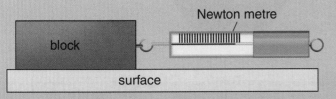

block

Newton metre

surface

He measures the force to pull a smooth wooden block over a smooth wooden surface. Then he measures the force to pull a sandpaper-covered block over a sandpaper-covered surface. He wants to make sure his results are accurate, so he repeats each reading three times and calculates an average value. He measures the size of his force in Newtons (N).

Surfaces	Force to pull block (N)			
	first time	second time	third time	average
rough sandpaper	11	10	9	10
smooth wood	5	7	6	

Callum writes a conclusion:

> The smoother the surfaces, the smaller the frictional force.

Have a go!

Make a parachute from string and a piece of plastic cut from an old bag. Can you make another parachute that falls more slowly?

Test yourself

1. What is friction?

2. Name three forces that act between moving surfaces.

3. Look again at the Working scientifically box. Calculate the average force to pull the block across the wood in Callum's experiment. Show how you worked out your answer.

4. Keira makes two parachutes to carry a model person. She drops them from the same height at the same time. Parachute A reaches the floor before parachute B. Which parachute experiences more air resistance?

Gravity

If you drop a ball, the Earth pulls it down. The force of **gravity** acts between the Earth and the ball.

The Earth pulls the ball down even though it is not touching the ball. Gravity is a **non-contact force**.

Magnets

In this picture, a **magnetic force** is pulling the magnets together. The magnets attract each other. The North Pole of one magnet is facing the South Pole of the other magnet.

If you turn one of the magnets round, they **repel** each other. Two magnets push away from each other when:

- their North Poles face each other
- their South Poles face each other.

Magnetic forces are **non-contact forces**. They can act even when they are not touching.

Magnets attract **magnetic materials**. They do not attract non-magnetic materials.

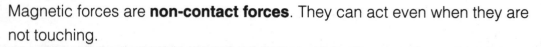

Magnetic materials	Non-magnetic materials
iron	aluminium
steel	copper
nickel	gold
cobalt	all materials that are not metals

Listen up 23

Gravity and magnets

Forces

Working scientifically

Comparing magnets

Catherine has two magnets. She wants to see which one is stronger. She counts the number of paper clips that hang in a chain from each magnet.

Catherine uses her results to make a prediction:

> Magnet B will hold more nails than magnet A.

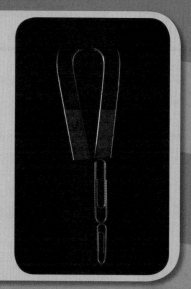

Keywords

Gravity ➤ The force between two objects. It pulls things towards the Earth

Magnetic force ➤ The force between two magnets, or between a magnet and a magnetic material

Repel ➤ Push away

Magnetic material ➤ A material that is attracted to a magnet

Have a go!

Walk around your home. Make a list of all the things you can find that include magnets.

Test yourself

1. What is gravity?
2. Underline the materials that are magnetic:

   copper   iron   wood

   steel   leather
3. Nathan holds two magnets close together, with their North Poles facing each other. Predict what will happen.
4. Look again at the Working scientifically box. Suggest how Catherine could find out if her prediction was correct.

Pulleys

A **pulley** is a **simple machine**. It makes lifting easier.

For example, pulleys are used by builders to help them lift heavy loads.

The pulley opposite has two wheels. Two sections of rope support the load. The force to lift the load with the pulley is half the force needed to lift the load without the pulley.

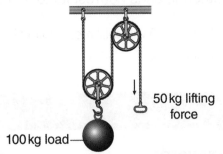

50 kg lifting force

100 kg load

Levers

A lever is a **simple machine**. It makes a small force have a big effect.

In this picture, a decorator uses a screwdriver to open the lid of a paint tin. The screwdriver is a **lever**. It applies a bigger force to the lid than you could apply with your hand.

Keywords

Pulley ➤ A system of wheels and ropes that make it easier to lift things

Simple machine ➤ A device that changes the direction or size of a force

Lever ➤ A straight rod with a pivot. You can use it to exert a big force over a small distance at one end by exerting a smaller force over a bigger distance at the other end

Listen up
24

Investigating levers

Lim asks a scientific question:

Is it easier to open a tin of paint with a short screwdriver or a long screwdriver?

Lim does an experiment to answer his question. The evidence shows that he needs to apply less force with a longer lever.

Gears

The **gear system** on a bike is a **simple machine**. You can choose a bigger or smaller cog on the back wheel to change gears.

Back cogs are usually smaller than front cogs. Back cogs turn faster than front cogs. The turning force of the back cog is smaller.

A bigger back cog turns more slowly than a smaller back cog. The turning force of a bigger cog is bigger than the turning force of a smaller cog. The bigger cog is better for going uphill.

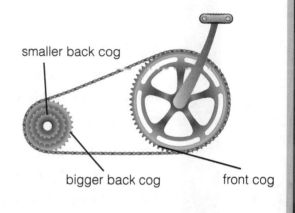

smaller back cog

bigger back cog   front cog

Keyword

Gear system ➤ A system of cogs that allows a small turning force to have a greater effect

Top tip! Levers, gear systems and pulleys are all simple machines.

Have a go! Try out Lim's investigation above. Ask an adult to help. Do you agree with his findings?

Test yourself
1. What is a simple machine?
2. Give examples of three types of simple machine.
3. Predict whether it is easier to open a paint tin using a coin or a screwdriver. Explain your prediction.

Making sounds

Sounds are made by **vibrating** objects.

For example:
- when you bang a drum, its skin vibrates
- when you play a ukulele, its strings vibrate.

Vibrating skins and strings make the air vibrate. The vibrations travel through the air. If the air vibrations enter your ear, you hear them as sounds.

Sound cannot travel through a vacuum, which is just empty space. It needs a **medium** to travel through, such as air, a liquid (such as water) or a solid (such as wood). You cannot hear sound in space.

Volume

Big, strong vibrations make loud sounds. For example, if you bang a drum hard, the vibrations are big and the drum makes a loud sound.

Small, weak vibrations make quiet sounds. For example, if you bang a drum gently, the vibrations are small and the drum makes a quiet sound.

The loudness of a sound is also called its **volume**. Turning up the volume makes a louder sound.

Next to a vibrating fire bell, the sound is very loud. As you move away from the sound source, the sound gets fainter.

Pitch

The **pitch** of a sound is how high or low it is. Pitch is nothing to do with loudness. A high-pitched sound can be loud or quiet. A low-pitched sound can be loud or quiet.

Listen up
25

Working scientifically

Investigating pitch

Clarice has a scientific question:

> How *does* the thickness of a guitar string affect the pitch of the sound?

Clarice plucks guitar strings of different thicknesses. She spots a pattern. The thicker the string, the lower the pitch.

Clarice investigates some more questions. She finds out that:

- the longer the string, the lower the pitch
- the tighter the string, the higher the pitch.

Keywords

Vibrating ➤ An object is vibrating if it is moving backwards and forwards again and again

Medium ➤ A material that sound travels through. A medium can be in the solid, liquid or gas state

Volume ➤ The loudness or quietness of a sound

Pitch ➤ How high or low a sound is

The investigation in **Have a go!** below demonstrates very clearly that sounds are made when an object (the speaker) vibrates.

Have a go!

With an adult, position a speaker so that its vibrations are vertical. Play some music, loudly. Place a few grains of *uncooked* rice on the speaker. Watch what happens.

Test yourself

❶ What must an object be doing in order to make a sound?

❷ Give examples of three materials that sound can travel through.

❸ What do you hear as you get further from a sound source?

❹ Predict which instrument makes sounds of lower pitch – a violin or a viola. Why? Use the pictures to help you.

violin

viola

Using electricity

How many electrical devices have you used today? Can you imagine life without mobile phones, computers and fridges?

Electrical circuits

In an electrical device, the electricity flows around a loop called a **circuit**. Electricity only flows if the circuit is complete. It must not have any gaps.

A simple circuit may include:

- a **cell** to push electricity around the circuit
- components such as bulbs, buzzers or motors
- wires to connect the cells and components
- a switch.

motor

cell

bulb

Note: people usually call a cell a battery. However, scientists say that a battery is two or more cells.

Symbols

You can use symbols to represent the components in a circuit.

Component	Symbol
cell	—‖—
bulb	—⊗—
buzzer	
motor	Ⓜ
wire	——
switch	—o o—

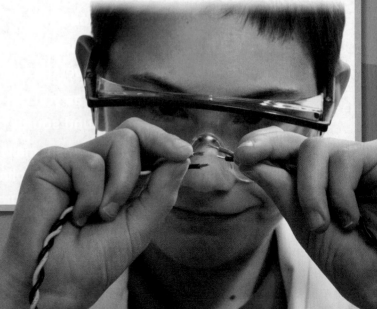

Listen up 26

Working scientifically

Conductors and insulators

Mo makes an electrical circuit with a gap. He wants to know which materials he can use to connect across the gap.

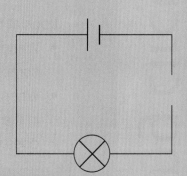

Mo tests different materials. The bulb lights when he connects copper or aluminium foil across the gap. It does not light when he connects wood or paper across the gap.

Mo uses his evidence to write a conclusion:

> Electricity flows through copper and aluminium.
> It does not flow through wood or paper.

Metals are good **conductors** of electricity. Most other materials are **electrical insulators**.

Keywords

Circuit ➤ Electricity flows around a complete circuit

Cell ➤ A cell pushes electricity around a complete circuit

Conductor ➤ A substance that electricity can flow through

Electrical insulator ➤ A substance that electricity cannot flow through

Top tip!

If you make a circuit and it doesn't work, check that there are no gaps in it. If it still doesn't work, test each component, one at a time, in another circuit that you know does work.

Have a go!

List all the electrical devices you can find at home.

Test yourself

❶ Draw the circuit symbol for a bulb.

❷ What happens if there is a gap in an electrical circuit?

❸ List two electrical conductors and two electrical insulators.

❹ Name the part of a mobile phone that pushes electricity around its circuits.

Switches

A **switch** turns a device on or off.

Look at this circuit.
- When the switch is closed (on), the circuit is complete. Electricity flows. The bulb lights.
- When the switch is open (off), there is a gap in the circuit. Electricity cannot flow. The bulb does not light.

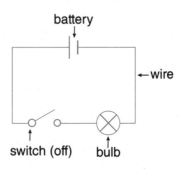

Brightness and loudness

In a circuit, the number of cells affects bulb brightness and buzzer loudness.

The cell **voltage** also makes a difference. The higher the voltage, the greater the 'push' that makes the electricity flow.

Circuits A and B below are almost identical, but circuit B has an extra cell. The bulb in circuit B is brighter.

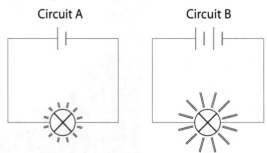

The cell in circuit D below has a higher voltage than the cell in circuit C. The buzzer in circuit D makes a louder sound.

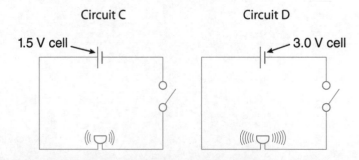

Keywords

Switch ➤ A component that turns a device on and off

Voltage ➤ The 'push' that makes electricity flow around a circuit

Working scientifically

Circuit investigation

Sophie investigates how the number of cells affects the loudness of a buzzer. She sets up this circuit.

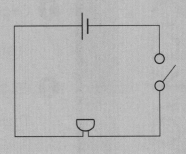

She designs a table for her results. She writes the variable she changes in the left-hand column, and the variable she observes in the right-hand column.

Number of cells	Buzzer loudness
1	quiet
2	medium
3	loud

Top tip! If your circuit is not working, check the switch. Is it closed?

Have a go! Use the Internet to find out about electrical safety. Search for 'electrical safety KS2'. Tell an adult what you have found out.

Test yourself

1. What is a switch?
2. Look at the Working scientifically box. Which variable does Sophie change in her investigation?
3. Look at the Working scientifically box. Write a conclusion for Sophie's investigation.
4. Give three reasons to explain why the bulb does not light in the circuit below.

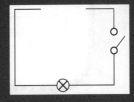

Classifying living things

❶ Circle **four** invertebrates. **(4 marks)**

snake   shark   bee   spider   ant   frog   snail   bat

❷ Fill in the gaps with the correct words. **(3 marks)**

There are two big groups of plants: non-flowering plants and

.... plants. Non-flowering plants include mosses and

.... Grasses are in the .... plants group.

❸ Write down **two** things that all birds have in common. **(2 marks)**

....

....

❹ There are about 60 000 different types of vertebrate. The chart shows the percentage of this number that are in each vertebrate group.

a. Which group has the biggest number of different types? **(1 mark)**

....

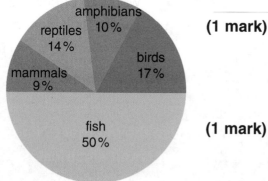

reptiles 14%
amphibians 10%
birds 17%
mammals 9%
fish 50%

b. Which group has the smallest number of different types? **(1 mark)**

....

❺ Use the key to find out which tree the leaf is from. Then circle the answer. **(1 mark)**

pine   horse chestnut   juniper   beech

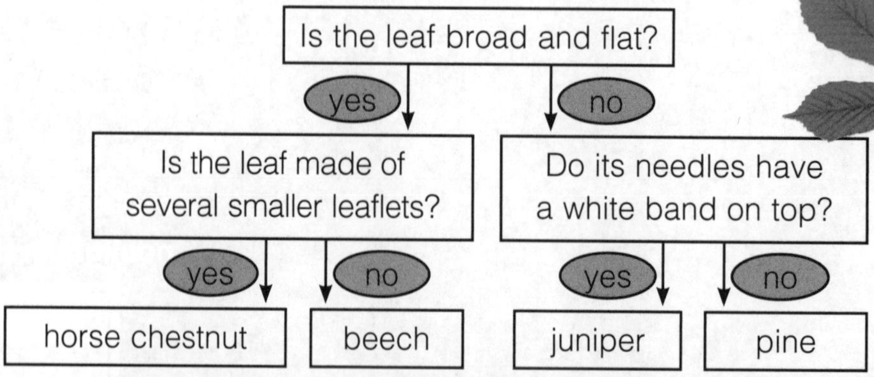

Is the leaf broad and flat?

yes → Is the leaf made of several smaller leaflets?
no → Do its needles have a white band on top?

Is the leaf made of several smaller leaflets?
yes → horse chestnut
no → beech

Do its needles have a white band on top?
yes → juniper
no → pine

Total 12

Plants

1) Fill in the gap with the correct word. **(1 mark)**

Plants need these things to grow: air, nutrients, light,

space and ....

2 Fill in the missing labels. **(2 marks)**

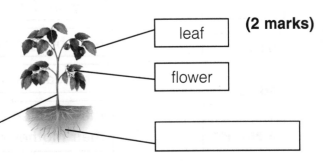

leaf

flower

3 What is the job of leaves? Tick the box next to the correct answer.

(1 mark)

a. support the plant ☐   **b.** make seeds ☐

c. take in nutrients ☐   **d.** make food ☐

4 Ollie adds different-coloured food dyes to jars of water. He puts a white flower in each jar. The next day he looks at his flowers. This is what he sees.

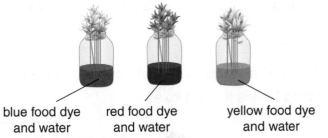

blue food dye
and water

red food dye
and water

yellow food dye
and water

a. Fill in the missing observation. **(1 mark)**

Colour of food dye	Observation
blue	flowers are ....
red	flowers are red
yellow	flowers are yellow

b. Which variable did Ollie change? .... **(1 mark)**

c. Explain why the flowers change colour. **(2 marks)**

....

....

Top tip! When there are two marks for a question, write about two things in your answer.

Total $\frac{}{8}$

Life cycles

❶ Draw lines to match each stage of the human life cycle with something that happens in that stage. **(4 marks)**

Stage	What happens
child	they are fully grown
baby	their body changes rapidly
adult	they learn to walk and talk
teenager	they feed on milk from their mother's breasts

❷ Tick the boxes next to the **two** animals that metamorphose. **(2 marks)**

bee ☐   ladybird ☐

horse ☐   whale ☐

❸ Write these words in the correct order for the life cycle of a butterfly, starting from the beginning of the life cycle. **(4 marks)**

pupa   egg   adult   larva

......................., ..., ..., ...

❹ The picture shows the stages in the life cycle of a frog. Write the missing labels in the boxes. **(4 marks)**

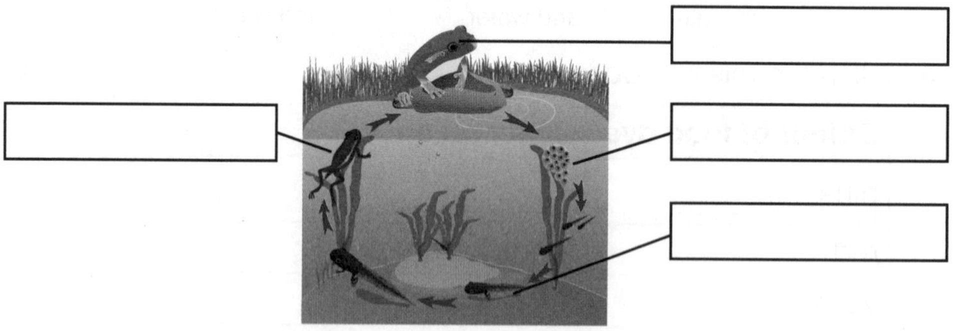

❺ Describe the life cycle of a chicken, starting with the egg. **(4 marks)**

....

....

....

Total 18

Reproduction

1 The text shows the stages in the sexual reproduction of a flowering plant.

Stage	What happens
pollination	pollen joins with ovules to make seeds
fertilisation	seeds move away from the plant
dispersal	pollen travels from the stamen of one flower to the stigma of another

a. Draw lines to match each stage with what happens in that stage. **(3 marks)**

b. Which **two** stages can animals help with? **(2 marks)**

....

2 The table shows the time from fertilisation to birth for five mammals.

Mammal	Time from fertilisation to birth (days)
cat	65
dog	60
mouse	20
rat	20
squirrel	35

Top tip! Do not forget to label the *x* and *y* axis of your chart.

a. On a separate piece of paper, draw a bar chart showing the data in the table. Write the mammal names on the *x* axis and the time from fertilisation to birth on the *y* axis. **(5 marks)**

b. This table gives some more data.

Mammal	Time from fertilisation to birth (days)	How heavy is the adult mammal (kg)?
cat	65	5
human	275	70
horse	335	500
sperm whale	535	55 000

Use the data in the table to complete the sentence below. **(1 mark)**

As the time from fertilisation to birth increases, ...

....

Total —— 11

Growing and Changing

Heart and blood

❶ Look at the diagram. Write the letter of the label that points to the heart. .... **(1 mark)**

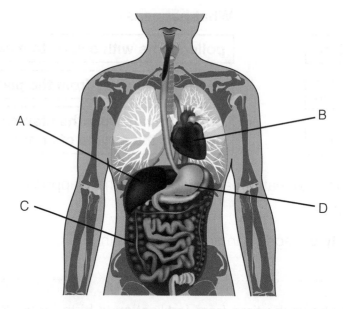

❷ Circle **three** things that blood carries around your body. **(3 marks)**

oxygen nutrients water urine saliva

❸ Katie measures the pulse rate of four friends. She measures the pulse of each friend three times.

Name	Pulse rate (beats per minute)			
	first time	second time	third time	average
Saniyah	80	85	75	
Rachel	180	170	160	170
Wilbur	69	79	74	74
Kieran	75	81	78	75

a. Calculate Saniyah's average pulse rate. **(2 marks)**

....

....

b. Who has been running? Give a reason for your choice. **(2 marks)**

Name: ....

Reason: ....

Total —8

Skeletons and muscles

1 What is your skeleton made of? .... **(1 mark)**

2 List the **three** jobs of the skeleton. **(3 marks)**

....

3 Here is a picture of an elephant skeleton.

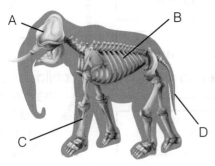

Parent tip! Make sure your child realises that mammal skeletons have many similarities. Ribs always protect organs such as the heart. The skull always protects the brain.

a. Write the letter which points to the ribs. .... **(1 mark)**

b. Write the letter which points to the skull. .... **(1 mark)**

c. What is the job of the skull? **(1 mark)**

....

4 Look at the two skeletons.

wolf   giraffe

a. List **two** similarities between the two skeletons. **(2 marks)**

....

....

b. List **two** differences between the two skeletons. **(2 marks)**

....

....

Total —— 11

Healthy living

1 Draw lines to match each food to its main nutrient. **(4 marks)**

Food	Nutrient
pasta	fat
chicken	carbohydrate
butter	vitamins and minerals
fruit	protein

Parent tip!

When you are eating with your child, discuss the main nutrients in different foods.

2 Circle the correct **bold** word in each pair. **(5 marks)**

The two nutrients whose main job is to provide you with energy are **carbohydrates/proteins** and **vitamins/fats**. The nutrients whose main job is to keep everything working properly are **vitamins/fat** and **carbohydrates/minerals**. The main nutrient that your body uses to repair damage is **protein/fat**.

3 What is a drug?
Tick the **best** answer. **(1 mark)**

A substance that affects how your body works. ☐

A substance that harms your body. ☐

A substance that makes you behave strangely. ☐

A substance that makes you better if you are ill. ☐

4 Alcohol is a drug. What effects can it have on a person?
Tick the **three** correct answers. **(3 marks)**

It can damage their heart. ☐

It might make them sick. ☐

It can damage their brain. ☐

It makes them drive more safely. ☐

Total ___ 13

Digestion

❶ Fill in the missing labels using the correct words. **(7 marks)**

| large intestine | stomach | small intestine |
| oesophagus | mouth | anus | rectum |

❷ What happens in each of these parts of the digestive system? **(3 marks)**

a. Mouth

....

b. Stomach

....

c. Anus

....

❸ Draw lines to match each type of tooth to its job. **(3 marks)**

Type of tooth   **Job**

| incisors | | tear food such as meat |

| canines | | grind and chew food |

| molars | | bite off pieces of food |

❹ Look at the skull in the picture. Do you think the animal ate mainly meat or mainly plants? Give a reason for your decision. **(2 marks)**

Answer: ....

Reason: ....

....

....

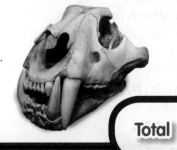

Total $\frac{}{15}$

Food chains

1 Look at this food chain.

grass   →   wildebeest   →   lion

a. What do the arrows mean? **(1 mark)**

....

b. Name the predator in the food chain. **(1 mark)**

....

c. Name the producer in the food chain. **(1 mark)**

....

d. Name the prey in the food chain. **(1 mark)**

....

2 Here is a seaside food chain.

seaweed   →   limpet   →   crab   →   seagull

a. Which animal in the food chain is both predator and prey? **(1 mark)**

....

b. Predict **two** things that might happen if people take lots
of crabs from the beach. **(2 marks)**

....

....

....

Remember,
producers make
their own food.
Prey are animals
eaten by other
animals. **Predators**
eat other
animals.

Top tip!

Total ——
7

Changing environments

1 Edward digs a pond in his garden.

Here is a food chain showing some of the living things in and around the pond.

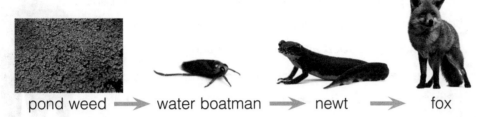

pond weed ➞ water boatman ➞ newt ➞ fox

a. Name the producer in the food chain. .... **(1 mark)**

b. Predict what might happen to the number of water boatmen in the pond if Edward removes the pond weed. **(1 mark)**

....

c. Edward buys a fox scarer for his garden. It makes a high-pitched sound that foxes do not like. The foxes move away from Edward's garden.

Predict what might happen to the number of newts in the pond.

.... **(1 mark)**

Explain your answer. **(1 mark)**

....

....

d. When the foxes go away, hedgehogs start eating the newts.
Draw a new food chain showing the pond weed, water boatman, newt and hedgehog. **(1 mark)**

Parent tip!

There are many possible answers to questions like these, because the animals in these food chains are also in other food chains. One food chain cannot give the complete picture.

Total $\dfrac{}{5}$

Evolution

❶ Read the information about elephants. Then complete
the table. **(4 marks)**

Adult elephants are huge, so other animals do not attack
them. They use their trunks to reach food high up in trees,
as well as to get food and water from the ground.

Their tusks are also useful. They use them to strip bark
from trees, which they then eat. They also use them to
dig to find water under dried-up rivers.

They flap their enormous ears to cool the blood in them.
The cooler blood then travels around their bodies.

Adaptation	How the adaptation helps them to survive
big size	
trunks	
tusks	
big ears	

❷ The steps below describe how head lice evolve, but they are in the
wrong order.

Write numbers next to each step to show the correct order. The first
one has been done for you. **(4 marks)**

A Individual head lice are not the same. They show variation.
`1`

B The surviving head lice lay eggs. The eggs hatch.
`☐`

C Some head lice have features which stop head lice shampoo
killing them. These head lice survive. The others die.
`☐`

D The steps are repeated. Eventually, all head lice have the
features that stop head lice shampoo killing them.
`☐`

E The offspring from the eggs are likely to have the features
that stop head lice shampoo killing them.
`☐`

Total — 8

Rocks and soil

1 Hilary has three rocks. She tries scratching them with different objects. The table shows her results.

Rock	Can I scratch it with my fingernail?	Can I scratch it with a knife?
A	yes	yes
B	no	yes
C	no	no

a. Which rock is easiest to scratch? .... **(1 mark)**

b. Which rock might be granite? .... **(1 mark)**

2 Riley has three different rocks, each of a different type. He weighs his rocks. Then he puts them in water. A week later he weighs the rocks again. His results are in the table.

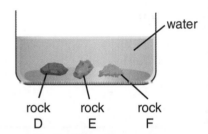

Rock	Mass of rock at start (g)	Mass of rock at end (g)	Mass of water that soaked into the rock (g)
D	50	59	9
E	50	50	0
F	50	67	

a. How much water soaked into rock F? Show your working. **(2 marks)**

....

....

b. Which rock is not porous? .... **(1 mark)**

c. Which rock is probably made up of crystals? .... **(1 mark)**

When you do a calculation, show how you work out the answer.

Top tip!

Total ——
6

Solid, liquid or gas?

❶ Fill in the gap with the correct word. **(1 mark)**

The three states of matter are solid, ... and gas.

❷ What is the name of solid water?
Tick the box next to the correct answer. **(1 mark)**

ice ☐   water vapour ☐

steam ☐   condensation ☐

❸ Fill in the table. **(4 marks)**

State	Can you squash it?	Does it flow?
gas	....	yes
liquid	....	....
....	no	no

❹ Seth has some water. He puts it in the freezer and it becomes solid. What change of state happens in the freezer? **(1 mark)**

....

❺ The table shows the melting temperatures of four materials.

Material	Melting temperature (°C)
copper	1083
gold	1063
iron	1535
silver	961

a. Which material in the table melts at the highest temperature?

.... **(1 mark)**

b. What is the difference between the melting points of copper and gold? Show your working. **(2 marks)**

....

....

Total $\frac{}{10}$

Water cycle

1 The diagram shows the water cycle. Fill in the gaps in the boxes.

(2 marks)

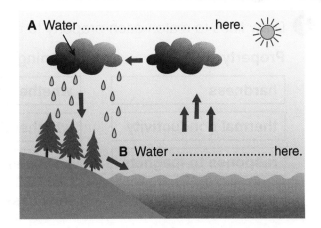

A Water .... here.

B Water .... here.

2 Circle the correct **bold** word in each pair. **(5 marks)**

The Sun **heats/cools** water in the sea. Some water **evaporates/condenses** to make water vapour. This rises and **heats/cools**. It **evaporates/condenses** to make liquid water in clouds. Liquid water falls from clouds as **rain/snow**.

3 Felix does an experiment to find out where water evaporates quickest. He puts some water on three different pieces of kitchen roll. He puts the pieces of kitchen roll in different places and leaves them for two hours.

a. What does Felix change in his investigation?

.... **(1 mark)**

b. How could Felix make his experiment fair?

.... **(1 mark)**

c. Draw lines to match each place to the most likely observation after two hours. **(3 marks)**

Place	Observation
on top of a heater	wet
in the playground (where it is cold and not raining)	dry
on a table inside	slightly damp

Total ── 12

States of Matter

Using materials

1 Draw lines to match each property to its meaning. **(4 marks)**

Property	Meaning
hardness	whether it is attracted to a magnet
thermal conductivity	whether it is see-through
response to magnets	how well heat travels through it
transparency	how easy or difficult it is to scratch

2 Which properties of copper make it suitable for electric cables?
Tick the boxes next to the **two** correct answers. **(2 marks)**

It is a good thermal conductor. ☐

It is shiny. ☐

It is a good electrical conductor. ☐

It is bendy. ☐

3 Circle the **two** materials that are magnetic. **(2 marks)**

      iron   **wood**   **gold**   **steel**

4 The table shows the hardness of some materials: the higher the number, the harder the material.

Draw a bar chart from the data in the table. **(4 marks)**

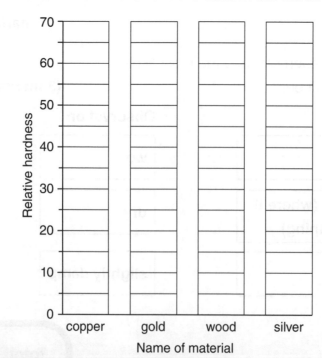

Material	Relative hardness
copper	70
gold	45
wood	5
silver	25

Total — 12

Mixtures

① Four children put some blue crystals in a glass.

They add water and stir. After stirring, there are no crystals. The picture shows what they see.

The children discuss their observations:

Top tip! It is easy to get **melting** and **dissolving** muddled up. Make sure you know the difference.

Max
The blue crystals have melted.

Roisin
The blue crystals have condensed.

Sunila
The blue crystals have evaporated.

Kassim
The blue crystals have dissolved.

Which child is correct? Write their name here. .... **(1 mark)**

② Marcus has a mixture of flour and sand.

Describe in detail how he could separate the mixture. **(4 marks)**

....

....

....

....

③ Fill in the gaps with the correct words. **(6 marks)**

solution	dissolves	soluble	filtering	dissolve

Harriet adds salt to water and stirs. The salt .... to

make a .... This shows that salt is ....
in water.

Then she gets another cup of water. She adds sand to the water.

The sand does not .... in water. It is not ....

You can separate sand and water by ....

Total 11

New materials

❶ Write **T** next to the statements that are true and **F** next to the statements that are false.　**(4 marks)**

A If a change is not reversible, it is easy to get the starting materials back again. ☐

B If a change is reversible, it is difficult to get the starting materials back again. ☐

C If a change is reversible, it is easy to get the starting materials back again. ☐

D If a change is not reversible, it is difficult to get the starting materials back again. ☐

❷ Circle the **three** non-reversible changes.　**(3 marks)**

burning　　melting　　condensing　　freezing

adding vinegar to bicarbonate of soda　　rusting

❸ Some children are talking about reversible changes and changes that are not reversible.

Barney
Dissolving sugar in tea is a reversible change.

Kamal
When you fry an egg, the changes are not reversible.

Simon
Making ice from water is not reversible.

Maya
Pouring sand into water is not reversible.

Add a tick (✓) or cross (✗) in the table to show whether each person is right or wrong.　**(4 marks)**

Name	Right or wrong?
Barney	....
Kamal	....
Simon	....
Maya	....

Total ── 11

How you see

1 Tick the **three** light sources. **(3 marks)**

Sun ☐   star ☐

television ☐   mirror ☐

Moon ☐   eyes ☐

2 You must never look directly at the Sun. Explain why. **(1 mark)**

....

3 Toby is reading a book with a torch. On the picture, draw one more arrow to show how he sees the book. **(1 mark)**

4 Circle the correct **bold** word in each pair to explain how you see a flower. **(5 marks)**

If you look at a flower outside, light from the Sun travels **to/from** the flower in a **curved/straight** line. The flower **blocks/reflects** the light. The **blocked/reflected** light travels to your **ear/eye**.

5 The man is having his hair cut. On the picture, draw one more arrow to show how the hairdresser sees the image of the man's hair in the mirror. Your arrow will cross over one of the arrows that is already there. **(1 mark)**

light ——

Make sure your child uses a ruler to draw straight arrows.

Parent tip!

Total $\frac{\quad}{11}$

Shadows

1 Look at the photo. Why does a shadow form when sunlight shines on the dog?
Tick the correct answer.

(1 mark)

The dog is transparent. ☐

The dog is moving. ☐

The dog is opaque. ☐

The dog is looking at its shadow. ☐

2 Circle the opaque materials. **(2 marks)**

glass   wood   gold   water

3 The shadow in the picture is short. The photo was taken in the middle of the day.

a. Explain why the shadow is short. **(1 mark)**

....

b. How would the shadow be different in the evening?
Explain your answer. **(2 marks)**

....

....

Parent tip!

Encourage your child to make shadows on sunny days. Ask them to work out how to change the size of the shadows, and to explain what they see.

Total —
6

Solar system

1 What is the shape of the Sun? .... **(1 mark)**

2 Write **T** next to the statements that are true and
F next to the statements that are false. **(5 marks)**

A   The Moon is a planet.

B   The Moon orbits the Earth.

C   The Moon's orbit takes 365 days.

D   There is one moon in our Solar System.

E   The Moon is crescent-shaped.

3 Lucy uses the Internet to find out some data about planets.
She writes the data in a table.

Planet	Distance of planet from Sun (million km)	Time to orbit Sun (Earth years)	Relative mass of planet compared to Earth (mass of Earth = 1)
Mercury	58	0.24	0.055
Venus	108	0.62	0.815
Earth	150	1.0	1.00
Mars	228	1.9	0.107
Jupiter	778	12	318
Saturn	1427	29	95.2
Uranus	2871	84	14.4
Neptune	4498	165	17.1

a. List the planets that have a smaller mass than Earth. **(3 marks)**

....

b. Which planet is furthest from the Sun? .... **(1 mark)**

c. Which planet takes the shortest time to orbit the Sun?

.... **(1 mark)**

d. Describe the relationship between the distance of the planet from
the Sun and the time to orbit the Sun. **(2 marks)**

....

....

Total $\dfrac{}{13}$

Day and night

❶ Circle the picture that represents the Earth rotating on its axis. **(1 mark)**

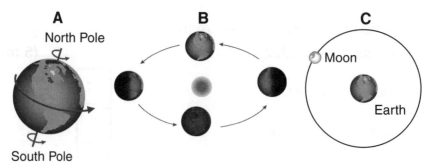

A

North Pole

South Pole

B

C

Moon

Earth

❷ Tick the box that shows how long it takes for the Earth to rotate on its axis. **(1 mark)**

1 year ☐　　1 week ☐　　1 month ☐　　1 day ☐

❸ Tick the box that gives the best scientific answer for what one day is. **(1 mark)**

From sunrise to sunset ☐

From midday to midnight ☐

From 06:00 one day to 06:00 the next day ☐

From 09:00 to 15:00 ☐

❹ a. Use the picture to help you explain why it is sometimes dark and sometimes light where you live. **(2 marks)**

....

....

....

b. If it is midday at spot A, at which spot would the time be closest to midnight? .... **(1 mark)**

A　C　D

B

Total ─── 6

Moving surfaces

1 Write **T** next to the statements that are true and **F** next
to the statements that are false. **(7 marks)**

A Pushes and pulls are forces.

B Friction tends to speed things up.

C Friction is a force.

D Friction tends to stop things moving.

E Friction is always a nuisance.

F Friction acts between surfaces if at least one of
the surfaces is moving.

G The smoother the surface, the greater the friction.

2 Reggie is investigating friction.
He measures the force to pull a shoe over three different surfaces.
His results are in the table.

Surface	Force to pull shoe (N)			
	first time	second time	third time	average
carpet	23	20	17	20
sandpaper	25	25	22	24
wood	16	19	16	

a. Suggest why Reggie tests each surface three times.

.... **(1 mark)**

b. Calculate the average force to pull the shoe over the wood. **(2 marks)**

....

....

c. On which surface is the frictional force
smallest? Explain how you know. **(2 marks)**

....

....

Parent tip!

Scientists repeat
tests and calculate
average values to
improve the accuracy
of their results.

Total $\frac{}{12}$

Gravity and magnets

1 Choose from the words below to complete the sentences.

> **non-contact**   **gravity**   **air resistance**
>
> **contact**   **magnetism**

Jake drops his shopping. The force of .... pulls it towards the Earth. The force acts on the shopping even though it is not touching the shopping. This shows that the force is a

.... force. **(2 marks)**

2 Draw circles around the materials that are magnetic. **(2 marks)**

iron   copper   steel   wood   paper

3 The blue object in the picture is a magnet. How do you think this magnet is useful in a car scrap yard? **(1 mark)**

....

4 How could Natasha use the paperclips to find out which of these magnets is stronger?

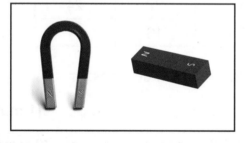 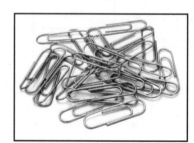

Write detailed instructions of the investigation she could do. **(3 marks)**

....

....

....

....

Total —— 8

Simple machines

1 Circle the correct **bold** word in each pair. **(2 marks)**

A man uses a crowbar to open a door. A crowbar is a type of
gear/lever. The further away from the door he holds the lever,
the **easier/harder** it is for him to open the door.

2 Give **three** examples of simple machines. **(3 marks)**

....

....

....

3 Fill in the gaps with the correct words. **(2 marks)**
Use the picture to help you.

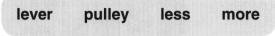

lever   pulley   less   more

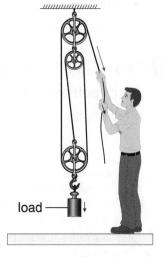

load

The weight is attached to a .... system. The force

needed to lift the load with this system is .... than

the force needed to lift the load without this system.

4 Caitlin attaches a handle to cog wheel **R**.
She uses the handle to turn the cog wheels.

R   **S**

a. Which cog wheel turns more slowly: **R** or **S**? .... **(1 mark)**

b. Which cog has the bigger turning force? .... **(1 mark)**

Total ___
9

Vibration, volume and pitch

1 Draw lines to match each word to its meaning.　　　**(3 marks)**

Word	Meaning
pitch	a material that sound travels through
volume	how high or low a sound is
medium	how loud or soft a sound is

2 Circle the correct **bold** word in each pair.　　　**(2 marks)**

A vibrating object makes a sound. The bigger the vibrations, the **quieter/louder** the sound. As you move away from the source of a sound, the sound appears to get **quieter/louder**.

3 Two children make an instrument out of bottles. They talk about their predictions.

Leo
When you hit the bottles with a spoon, the bottle with most water will have the lowest pitch.

Paige
When you bang the bottles with a spoon, the one with the most water in it will sound loudest.

a. Explain why Paige is not correct.　　　**(1 mark)**

....

....

b. Use ideas about vibrations to explain why Leo is correct.　　**(1 mark)**

....

....

....

....

Total —7

Making circuits

❶ Add circuit symbols and words to complete the table.　　**(6 marks)**

Component	Circuit symbol
cell	....
....	Ⓜ
bulb	....
wire	....
....	⯊
....	—o⁄ o—

❷ Complete the sentences below.　　**(2 marks)**

In a torch, the electricity flows around a ....

Electricity only flows if this is ....

❸ Write each material in the correct column of the table.　　**(9 marks)**

> copper　　aluminium　　plastic　　wood　　silver
> paper　　cardboard　　glass　　iron

Conductors	Insulators

❹ Explain why the bulb does not light in the circuit below.　　**(1 mark)**

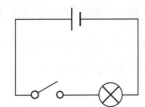

....

Total $\frac{}{18}$

Changing circuits

❶ Oscar sets up circuit A with one bulb and one cell.
Then he adds another cell to make circuit B.

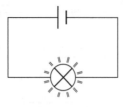

Circuit A   Circuit B

a. Is the bulb brighter in circuit A or circuit B? .... **(1 mark)**

b. Explain your answer to part **a.** **(1 mark)**

....

....

❷ Olivia asks a scientific question:
How does the number of bulbs in a
circuit affect their brightness?

She sets up the circuit below.

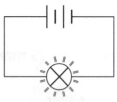

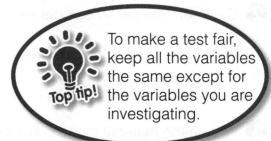

To make a test fair, keep all the variables the same except for the variables you are investigating.

Top tip!

She adds two more bulbs and records their brightness in a table.

....	Brightness
1	most bright
2	less bright
3	least bright

a. Write down **one** thing she must do to make the

investigation fair. .... **(1 mark)**

b. Write the missing column heading in the table. **(1 mark)**

❸ Use the results in the table to describe the relationship between the
number of bulbs and their brightness. **(2 marks)**

....

....

Total ⎯ 6

1 Alison wants to grow tomato plants in her garden.

a. She tests the soil in different parts of her garden. She draws pie charts to display her results.

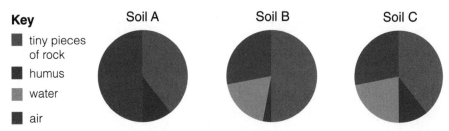

Key
- ■ tiny pieces of rock
- ■ humus
- ■ water
- ■ air

Soil A   Soil B   Soil C

i. Why will the plants not grow well in soil A? **(1 mark)**

....

ii. Humus is made up of tiny pieces of dead plants and animals.
Tomato plants grow well in humus-rich soil.
Which soil is best for growing tomatoes: A, B or C? .... **(1 mark)**

b. The diagram shows a tomato plant.

Tick the **two** parts of the plant that support it. **(2 marks)**

roots ☐   flowers ☐

stem ☐   leaves ☐

c. Alison notices aphids eating the leaves of her tomato plants.
Here is a food chain that includes aphids.

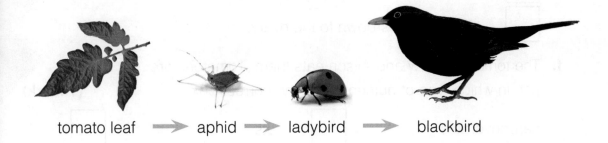

tomato leaf → aphid → ladybird → blackbird

i. Name the producer in the food chain. .... **(1 mark)**

ii. Alison wants ladybirds to come to her garden.
Suggest why. **(1 mark)**

....

....

iii. Name two predators in the food chain.

.... and .... **(2 marks)**

d. The diagram shows a tomato flower.
Fill in the **two** missing labels. **(2 marks)**

A [ ]

stamen

B [ ]

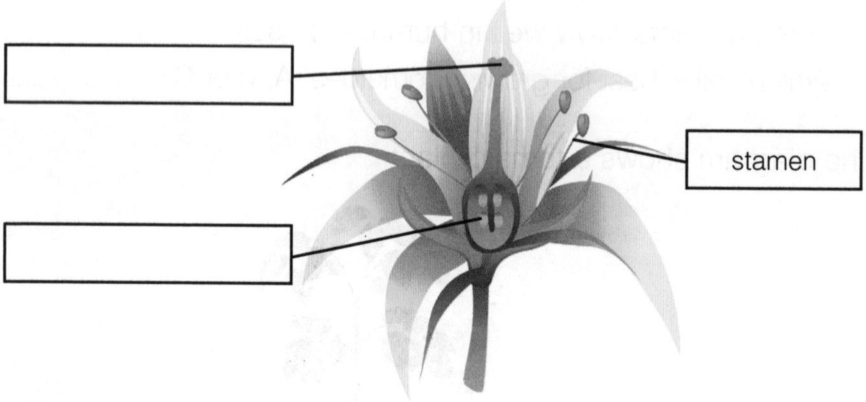

e. The steps below describe how the tomato flowers produce seeds, but
they are in the wrong order.
Write a number next to each step to show the correct order. The first one
has been done for you. **(4 marks)**

| 1 | Pollen travels from the stamen to stigma. |

[ ] This is fertilisation.

[ ] Pollen joins with ovules to make seeds.

[ ] This is pollination.

[ ] Pollen moves down to the ovary.

f. The tomatoes grow and Alison eats them. Tomatoes are
rich in which type of nutrient? Tick the correct box. **(1 mark)**

carbohydrates [ ]   fats [ ]

protein [ ]   vitamins and minerals [ ]

2 Roisin is investigating ice. She puts ice cubes on plates.

She uses her watch to measure the time it takes for the ice to melt.
Her results are in the table.

Number of ice cubes	Time to melt (minutes)
1	128
2	137
4	142
8	163

a. Describe the relationship between the number of ice
cubes and the time it takes for them to melt. **(2 marks)**

....

....

b. Describe **one** thing that Roisin should do to make her
investigation fair. **(1 mark)**

....

....

c. Complete the sentences.

Ice .... to make liquid water. If you put
the water in the freezer, it will freeze to form ice again.

Ice is water in the .... state. **(2 marks)**

d. Miss Davies gives Roisin an ice cube with sand mixed
up in it. She asks Roisin to give her some dry sand from
the mixture at the end of the week.

Write step-by-step instructions to tell Roisin what to do. In
your answer, include the names of **two** changes of state
and **one** separation technique. **(3 marks)**

....

....

....

....

3 Afiba lives in Nigeria. One day the Moon comes between the Earth and the Sun. Afiba cannot see the Sun for a few minutes.

a. Choosing from the words below, fill in the gaps with the correct words. **(5 marks)**

| star   transparent   planet   **Earth**   **Sun**   opaque   **Moon** |

The Sun is a .... The Earth is a .... The

Earth orbits the .... The Moon orbits the ....

The Moon is ....

b. The red arrows show rays of light from the Sun.

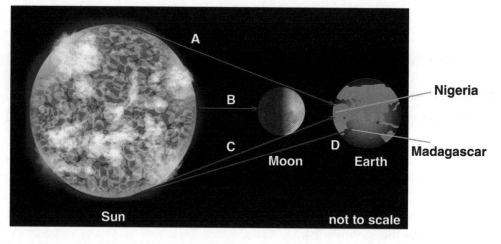

i. Use arrow B to explain why there is a shadow of the Moon on the Earth. **(2 marks)**

....

....

....

ii. What is the shape of the Moon's shadow on the Earth?

.... **(1 mark)**

iii. Haja lives in Madagascar. Use arrow D to explain why he can see the Sun. **(2 marks)**

....

....

iv. Why must you never look directly at the Sun? **(1 mark)**

....

REVISION GUIDE

VARIETY OF LIFE

page 5

1. Plants make their own food.
2. An animal with a bony skeleton, including a backbone.
3. mammals, birds, fish, amphibians, reptiles
4. insects and spiders
5. worm

page 7

1. air, water, nutrients, light, space
2. The flower makes seeds.
3. roots and stem
4. Leaves take in carbon dioxide from the air. They use carbon dioxide and water to make food for the plant.

GROWING AND CHANGING

page 9

1. When an animal changes completely as it grows.
2. **Any reasonable examples**, including butterfly or ladybird (insects) and frog (amphibian).
3. frog spawn, tadpole, froglet, frog
4. egg, larva (caterpillar), pupa (chrysalis), adult butterfly

page 11

1. Making a new living thing.
2. one
3. Pollination is the transport of pollen from one flower to another; fertilisation is the joining of pollen with ovules to make seeds.
4. The bird eats the berries. It does not digest the seed, which comes out of its body in its faeces. The seed can then grow.

YOUR BODY

page 13

1. heart, blood and blood vessels
2. pumps blood around the body
3. **Any two from:** nutrients, oxygen, waste substances.
4. Any answer above 150 beats per minute.

page 15

1. The structure of bones in a body.
2. support, movement and protection
3. **Any named five animals from these groups:** mammals, birds, fish, amphibians and reptiles.
4. In order to bend your elbow upwards, your biceps muscle contracts. It pulls up the bone it is joined to at the bottom of your arm. At the same time, the other muscle underneath your arm is relaxed.

page 17

1. carbohydrates, fats, proteins, vitamins and minerals
2. **Any two foods that are high in fat:** for example, chips, cakes, cheese, butter, oil
3. heart, stomach, brain, liver
4. alcohol and tobacco

page 19

1. To break down food so your body can absorb it.
2. Digestive juices start to digest food in the stomach.
3. Avoid sugary food and drinks, brush your teeth twice a day, go to the dentist for check-ups.

4. Incisors are flat and molars are wider with a rough surface. This means that incisors are suitable for biting off pieces of food and molars are suitable for chewing and grinding.

WEB OF LIFE

page 21

1. A living thing that makes its own food; a plant.
2. **a** snail and frog
   b frog
3. grass ⟶ zebra ⟶ lion

page 23

1. The surroundings of a plant or animal that supplies everything that the plant or animal needs.
2. The number of foxes will decrease.
3. There is less ice, so it is harder for polar bears to hunt and find prey animals like seals. The distances between ice platforms are greater, making swimming between them more perilous.

page 25

1. **Accept any sensible suggestion**, including different-coloured eyes, different-coloured hair, more or fewer freckles, and so on.
2. The eagle has sharp talons for grasping and carrying off its prey, and a sharp beak for catching its prey and tearing its flesh.
3. The plants or animals that are produced by their parent or parents.
4. The development of plants or animals over many years.

EARTH

page 27

1. The preserved remains or traces of an animal or plant that lived many years ago.
2. A rock that water can soak into.
3. tiny pieces of rock, dead plants and dead animals, air and water
4. Crystals, because it is hard and non-porous.

STATES OF MATTER

page 29

1. solid, liquid, gas
2. melting
3. **Accept two from:** The shape of a solid does not change unless you apply a force, but a liquid takes the shape of the bottom of the container it is in. You can hold a solid but you cannot easily hold a liquid. You can pour a liquid but you cannot usually pour a solid.

page 31

1. evaporation
2. condensation
3. It will evaporate more quickly in Dar es Salaam
4. Water evaporates from the oceans and other bodies of water. It rises through the atmosphere. High above Earth it condenses to form clouds, then falls as rain for drinking and to water crops, etc.

MIXING AND MAKING

page 33

1. A material that lets light through and that you can see through.
2. **Four from:** Wood is opaque. It is an electrical insulator. It is a thermal insulator. It is not magnetic. It is softer than steel.
3. diamond

page 35

1 A mixture is made up of two or more materials. It is often easy to separate the materials in a mixture.
2 **Any three from:** melting, freezing, evaporating, condensing, dissolving.
3 evaporation
4 Water can pass through the tiny holes, but sand cannot. This means that sand remains in the filter paper and water passes through into the container below.

page 37

1 A variable you keep the same in a fair test.
2 burning <u>melting</u> rusting <u>dissolving</u>
3 In a change that is reversible you can get back the original materials; no new materials are made. In a change that is not reversible it is difficult – or impossible – to get the starting materials back again; one or more new materials are made.
4 Not reversible. You cannot get the untoasted bread back again.

LIGHT

page 39

1 **Five from this list, or other suitable answers:** Sun, other stars, lamps, torches, candles, computer screens, television.
2 mirror
3

4 190 cm − 150 cm = 40 cm

page 41

1 An area of darkness on a surface caused by an opaque object blocking out light.
2 You can see through a transparent object because light passes through it. You cannot see through an opaque material because light does not pass through it.
3 **One from:** lamp, block of wood, ruler.
4 By moving it closer to the lamp or moving the lamp closer to it.

SPACE

page 43

1 Sun
2 Earth
3 **One from:** They are all roughly spherical. They are all part of the same solar system.
4 The Earth orbits the Sun but the Moon orbits the Earth.

page 45

1 24 hours
2 towards the east
3 When the part of the Earth you are on faces the Sun, it is light. When the part of the Earth you are on faces away from the Sun, it is dark.
4 The Earth moves towards the east, so we see the Sun rise in the east in the morning and set in the west in the evening.

FORCES

page 47

1 A force that acts between surfaces and slows down or stops things that are moving.
2 friction, air resistance, water resistance
3 5N + 7N + 6N = 18N
   18N ÷ 3 = 6N
4 parachute B

page 49

1 The force between two objects. It pulls things towards the Earth.
2 copper <u>iron</u> wood <u>steel</u> leather
3 The poles will push each other apart – they will repel each other.
4 She could repeat the investigation with steel nails instead of paper clips.

page 51

1 A device that changes the direction or size of a force.
2 pulley, gear, lever
3 A screwdriver because you need to apply less force if the lever is longer.

SOUND

page 53

1 It must vibrate.
2 **Any three reasonable answers**, including air, water, wood.
3 The sound gets quieter.
4 viola; larger size

ELECTRICITY

page 55

1

2 Electricity does not flow through the circuit, so the components do not work.
3 **Conductors – any two correct answers**, including copper and iron; **insulators – any two correct answers**, including wood and plastic.
4 cell or battery

page 57

1 A component that turns a device on and off.
2 the number of cells
3 The greater the number of cells, the louder the buzzer.
4 The bulb does not light because there is a gap in the circuit, there is no cell/battery and the switch is open/off.

WORKBOOK

VARIETY OF LIFE

page 58

1 snake shark (bee) (spider) (ant) frog (snail) bat   **(4 marks)**
2 There are two big groups of plants: non-flowering plants and **flowering** plants. Non-flowering plants include mosses and **ferns/conifer trees**. Grasses are in the **flowering** plants group.
                                                                                               (3 marks)
3 **Accept two from:** feathers, wings, lay eggs.
                                                                                               (2 marks)
4 a fish   **(1 mark)**
   b mammals   **(1 mark)**
5 (horse chestnut)   **(1 mark)**

page 59
1 water (1 mark)
2 **From left to right:** stem, roots. (2 marks)

3 **d** make food ✓ (1 mark)
4 **a** blue (1 mark)
  b colour of food dye (1 mark)
  c The stem transports the different-coloured water to the flowers. (1 mark) When the different-coloured water reaches the flower, the flower gradually changes colour. (1 mark)

GROWING AND CHANGING

page 60
1 child – they learn to walk and talk; baby – they feed on milk from their mother's breasts; adult – they are fully grown; teenager – their body changes rapidly **(4 marks: award 1 mark for each correct match)**
2 bee ✓ (1 mark)

  ladybird ✓ (1 mark)

3 egg, larva, pupa, adult (4 marks)
4 **Clockwise from top right:** frog, frog spawn, tadpole, froglet **(4 marks: award 1 mark for each correct label)**.
5 **Include these points:** an adult chicken lays an egg **(1 mark)**. If the female has mated with a male, a chick develops inside the egg **(1 mark)**. After a few weeks, the chick hatches **(1 mark)**. It grows into a chicken **(1 mark)**.

page 61
1 **a** pollination – pollen travels from the stamen of one flower to the stigma of another; fertilisation – pollen joins with ovules to make seeds; dispersal – seeds move away from the plant. **(3 marks: award 1 mark for each correct match)**
  b pollination and dispersal (2 marks)
2 **a**
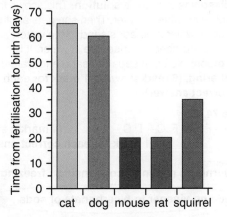
Mammal
  (5 marks: award 1 mark for each correct bar)
  b As the time from fertilisation to birth increases, **the adult animal gets heavier.** (1 mark)

YOUR BODY

page 62
1 B (1 mark)
2 (oxygen) (nutrients)
  (water) urine saliva (3 marks)

3 **a** 80 + 85 + 75 = 240 (1 mark)
  240 ÷ 3 = 80 beats per minute (1 mark)
  (Award only 1 mark for correct calculation but wrong answer.)
  b Rachel **(1 mark)**; her heart rate is much higher than anyone else's **(1 mark)**.

page 63
1 bones (1 mark)
2 support **(1 mark)**, protection **(1 mark)**, movement **(1 mark)**. **Answers can be in any order.**
3 **a** B (1 mark)
  b A (1 mark)
  c to protect the brain (1 mark)
4 **a** **Accept any two reasonable answers, including:** they both have ribs, they both have skulls, they both have bones in their necks, they both have a backbone **(2 marks: award 1 mark for each correct answer)**
  b **Accept any two reasonable answers, including:** the wolf has shorter bones in its neck; the wolf has shorter bones in its legs **(2 marks: award 1 mark for each correct answer)**

page 64
1 pasta – carbohydrate; chicken – protein; butter – fat; fruit – vitamins and minerals **(4 marks: award 1 mark for each correct match)**
2 The two nutrients whose main job is to provide you with energy are (carbohydrates) and (fats). The nutrients whose main job is to keep everything working properly are (vitamins) and (minerals). The main nutrient that your body uses to repair damage is (protein). **(5 marks)**
3 A substance that affects how your body works. ✓ (1 mark)
4 It can damage their heart. ✓
  It might make them sick. ✓
  It can damage their brain. ✓ (3 marks)

page 65
1
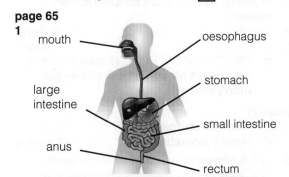
  (7 marks: award 1 mark for each correct answer)
2 **a** Your tongue detects taste and teeth chew food. Saliva starts to break down food. **(1 mark)**
  b Chewed food mixes with digestive juices; food starts to break down. **(1 mark)**
  c Faeces leave your body. **(1 mark)**
3 incisors – bite off pieces of food; canines – tear food such as meat; molars – grind and chew food **(3 marks: award 1 mark for each correct match)**
4 Answer: meat **(1 mark)** Reason: It has huge canines to tear food. **(1 mark)**

WEB OF LIFE

page 66

1 a is eaten by **(1 mark)**
   b lion **(1 mark)**
   c grass **(1 mark)**
   d wildebeest **(1 mark)**
2 a crab **(1 mark)**
   b **Accept two from:** the number of limpets will increase, the number of seagulls will decrease, the amount of seaweed will decrease. **(2 marks: award 1 mark for each correct reason)**

page 67

1 a pond weed **(1 mark)**
   b The number will decrease. **(1 mark)**
   c They will increase **(1 mark)** because there are fewer foxes to eat them. **(1 mark)**
   d pond weed ⟶ water boatman ⟶ newt ⟶ hedgehog **(1 mark)**

page 68

1 big size – it stops other animals killing them; trunks – they can reach high-up food, and drink water from low down; tusks – helps them to strip bark from trees to eat, and dig to find water under dried-up rivers; big ears – helps them to cool down **(4 marks)**
2 1A, 2C, 3B, 4E, 5D **(4 marks: award 1 mark for each correct answer)**

EARTH

page 69

1 a A **(1 mark)**
   b C **(1 mark)**
2 a 67 g – 50 g **(1 mark)** = 17 g **(1 mark)**
   b E **(1 mark)** c E **(1 mark)**

STATES OF MATTER

page 70

1 liquid **(1 mark)**
2 ice **(1 mark)**
3 Gas: **yes**, yes; liquid: **no, yes**; solid: no, no **(4 marks: award 1 mark for each correct answer)**
4 freezing **(1 mark)**
5 a iron **(1 mark)**
   b 1083 °C – 1063 °C = 20 °C **(2 marks: award only 1 mark for correct calculation but wrong answer)**

page 71

1 A – Water **condenses** here.
   B – Water **evaporates** here. **(2 marks)**
2 The Sun (heats) water in the sea. Some water (evaporates) to make water vapour. This rises and (cools). It (condenses) to make liquid water in clouds. Liquid water falls from clouds as (rain). **(5 marks: award 1 mark for each correct answer)**
3 a The place he leaves the kitchen roll. **(1 mark)**
   b By putting the same amount of water on each piece of kitchen roll. **(1 mark)**
   c On top of a heater – dry; in the playground (where it is cold and not raining) – wet; on a table inside – slightly damp **(3 marks: award 1 mark for each correct match)**

MIXING AND MAKING

page 72

1 hardness – how easy or difficult it is to scratch; thermal conductivity – how well heat travels through it; response to magnets – whether it is attracted to a magnet; transparency – whether it is see-through **(4 marks: award 1 mark for each correct match)**

2 It is a good electrical conductor. ☑

   It is bendy. ☑ **(2 marks)**
3 (iron) wood gold (steel) **(2 marks)**
4

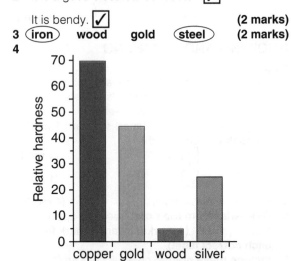

(4 marks: award 1 mark for each correct bar)

page 73

1 Kassim **(1 mark)**
2 Put the mixture in a sieve with holes that are smaller than the grains of sand but bigger than the tiny pieces of flour **(1 mark)**. Move the sieve quickly from side to side **(1 mark)**. The flour will come through the sieve. You can collect it in a container below the sieve **(1 mark)**. The sand will remain in the sieve **(1 mark)**.
3 Harriet adds salt to water and stirs. The salt **dissolves** to make a **solution**. This shows that salt is **soluble** in water. Then she gets another cup of water. She adds sand to the water. The sand does not **dissolve** in water. It is not **soluble**. You can separate sand and water by **filtering**. **(6 marks: award 1 mark for each correct answer)**

page 74

1 A – F, B – F, C – T, D – T **(4 marks: award 1 mark for each correct answer)**

2 (burning) melting condensing freezing

   (adding vinegar to bicarbonate of soda)

   (rusting) **(3 marks)**
3 Barney: right; Kamal: right; Simon: wrong; Maya: wrong. **(4 marks: award 1 mark for each correct 'right or wrong' answer)**

LIGHT

page 75

1 Sun ☑ star ☑ television ☑ **(3 marks)**
2 It is very bright and can damage your eyes. **(1 mark)**

3 (1 mark)

4 If you look at a flower outside, light from the Sun travels (to) the flower in a (straight) line. The flower (reflects) the light. The (reflected) light travels to your (eye). **(5 marks: award 1 mark for each correct answer)**

5 (1 mark)

page 76

1 The dog is opaque. ☑ (1 mark)

2 glass (wood) (gold) water **(2 marks)**

3 a The Sun is high in the sky, it is overhead. **(1 mark)**

   b The shadow would be longer **(1 mark)** because the Sun is lower in the sky **(1 mark)**.

SPACE

page 77

1 spherical **(1 mark)**

2 A – F, B – T, C – F, D – F, E – F **(5 marks: award 1 mark for each correct answer)**

3 a Mercury **(1 mark)**, Venus **(1 mark)**, Mars **(1 mark)**

   b Neptune **(1 mark)**

   c Mercury **(1 mark)**

   d As the distance of the planet from the Sun increases **(1 mark)**, the time to orbit the Sun increases **(1 mark)**.

page 78

1 **A** should be circled **(1 mark)**

2 1 day ☑ **(1 mark)**

3 From 06:00 one day to 06:00 the next day ☑ **(1 mark)**

4 a When you are in the half of the Earth that is facing the Sun, it is light **(1 mark)**. When the Earth rotates and you are in the half of the Earth that is not facing the Sun, it is dark **(1 mark)**.

   b D **(1 mark)**

FORCES

page 79

1 A – T, B – F, C – T, D – T, E – F, F – T, G – F **(7 marks: award 1 mark for each correct answer)**

2 a to improve the accuracy of his results **(1 mark)**

   b 16 N + 19 N + 16 N = 51 N **(1 mark)**
   51 N ÷ 3 = 17 N **(1 mark)**

   c The frictional force is smallest on the wood **(1 mark)**, where the force to pull the shoe is smallest at only 17 N **(1 mark)**.

page 80

1 Jake drops his shopping. The force of **gravity** pulls it towards the Earth. The force acts on the shopping even though it is not touching the shopping. This shows that the force is a **non-contact** force. **(2 marks)**

2 (iron) copper (steel) wood paper **(2 marks)**

3 It separates iron and steel objects from objects made out of other materials. **(1 mark)**

4 Add paper clips, in a line, to each magnet in turn **(1 mark)**. Count the number of paper clips that each magnet can hold **(1 mark)**. The one that can hold more paper clips is stronger **(1 mark)**.

page 81

1 A man uses a crowbar to open a door. A crowbar is a type of (lever). The further away from the door he holds the lever, the (easier) it is for him to open the door. **(2 marks)**

2 pulleys **(1 mark)**, levers **(1 mark)**, gears **(1 mark)**

3 The weight is attached to a **pulley** system. The force needed to lift the load with this system is **less** than the force needed to lift the load without this system. **(2 marks)**

4 a R **(1 mark)**

   b R **(1 mark)**

SOUND

page 82

1 pitch – how high or low a sound is; volume – how loud or soft a sound is; medium – a material that sound travels through **(3 marks: award 1 mark for each correct match)**

2 A vibrating object makes a sound. The bigger the vibrations, the (louder) the sound. As you move away from the source of a sound, the sound appears to get (quieter). **(2 marks)**

3 a The amount of water in the bottle affects the pitch of the sound, not its loudness. **(1 mark)**

   b Leo is correct because when you hit the bottles with the spoon, the water and the glass vibrates. The more water, the lower the pitch. **(1 mark)**

ELECTRICITY

page 83

1 cell: ⊣⊢; **motor:** (M); **bulb:** ⊗;

wire: ——————; **buzzer:** ⊔;

switch (open): —o o—
(6 marks: award 1 mark for each correct symbol/word)

2 In a torch, the electricity flows around a **circuit**. Electricity only flows if this is **complete**. **(2 marks)**

3 **Conductors:** copper, aluminium, silver, iron.
Insulators: plastic, wood, paper, cardboard, glass. **(9 marks: award 1 mark for each correct answer)**

4 The switch is off/open. **(1 mark)**

page 84

1 a circuit B **(1 mark)**

   b Circuit B has more cells, so there is a greater 'push' to make the electricity go around the circuit. **(1 mark)**

Answers

2 a keep the same cells in the circuit **(1 mark)**
b number of bulbs **(1 mark)**
3 As the number of bulbs increases **(1 mark)**, their brightness decreases **(1 mark)**.

MIXED PRACTICE QUESTIONS
pages 85–88

1 a i There is no water in the soil. **(1 mark)**
ii C **(1 mark)**

b roots ☑ stem ☑ **(2 marks)**

c i tomato leaf **(1 mark)**
ii To remove the aphids, or reduce their number, by eating them. **(1 mark)**
iii ladybird **(1 mark)**, blackbird **(1 mark)**

d A: stigma
B: ovule **(2 marks)**

e **2** – This is pollination. **3** – Pollen moves down to the ovary. **4** – Pollen joins with ovules to make seeds. **5** – This is fertilisation. **(4 marks)**

f vitamins and minerals ☑ **(1 mark)**

2 a As the number of ice cubes increase **(1 mark)**, the time taken to melt increases **(1 mark)**.
b The plates should all be in the same part of the room so that the temperature is the same. **(1 mark)**

c Ice **melts** to make liquid water. If you put the water in the freezer, it will freeze to form ice again. Ice is water in the **solid** state. **(2 marks)**
d Allow the ice to **melt** (change of state) **(1 mark)**. **Filter** (separation technique) the sandy mixture **(1 mark)**. Place the damp sand in a warm place so the water can **evaporate** (change of state) from it **(1 mark)**.

3 a The Sun is a **star**. The Earth is a **planet**. The Earth orbits the **Sun**. The Moon orbits the **Earth**. The Moon is **opaque**. **(5 marks)**
b i Arrow B shows light from the Sun reaching the Moon, but it can travel no further because the Moon is opaque **(1 mark)**. This light does not reach the Earth **(1 mark)**.
ii round/circular **(1 mark)**
iii Arrow D shows light from the Sun reaching the Earth at Madagascar **(1 mark)**. It is not blocked by an opaque object **(1 mark)**. This is why Haja can see the Sun.
iv You can damage your eyesight. **(1 mark)**

Glossary

Adaptations – The features of an animal or plant that help it to survive in its environment
Air resistance – A force that slows things down in air
Asexual reproduction – Making a new plant without seeds
Axis – An imaginary line between the North Pole and the South Pole, going through the centre of the Earth
Blood – Blood is mainly water with dissolved nutrients. It also includes red blood cells
Blood vessels – The tubes that blood flows through
Carbohydrates – Nutrients that provide energy
Cell – A cell pushes electricity around a complete circuit
Circuit – Electricity flows around a complete circuit
Circulatory system – The circulatory system includes the heart, blood vessels and blood. It transports nutrients and oxygen around the body
Classification key – A series of questions to help you identify a living thing
Classify – To sort living things into groups depending on their similarities and differences
Conclusion – What you have found out in an investigation
Condense – The change of state from gas to liquid
Conductivity – How easy it is for electricity or heat to travel through a material. The higher the value for electrical conductivity of a material, the more easily electricity travels through it

Conductor – A substance that electricity can flow through
Contract – When a muscle contracts, it becomes short and fat
Control variables – The variables you keep the same in a fair test
Crystal – A piece of solid material with a regular shape and flat faces
Digestive system – Your digestive system breaks down food so that your body can use it
Dissolving – Mixing a solid with a liquid to make a solution
Drugs – Substances that affect how your body works
Electrical insulator – A substance that electricity cannot flow through
Environment – The surroundings of a plant or animal. It supplies everything the plant or animal needs
Evaporate – The change of state from liquid to gas
Evolution – The development of plants or animals over many years
Fair test – An investigation where you keep all the variables the same except the ones that you are changing and measuring
Fats – Nutrients that provide energy. Your body can store them
Fertilisation – The joining of pollen with ovules to make seeds in plants, or the joining of a sperm with an egg in animals
Food chain – A diagram that shows what eats what

Forces – Forces can change the movement and shapes of objects

Fossil – The preserved remains or traces of an animal or plant that lived many years ago

Freezing – The change of state from liquid to solid

Friction – A force that acts between surfaces and slows down or stops things that are moving

Gear system – A system of cogs that allows a small turning force to have a greater effect

Grain – A small piece of a solid material that does not have a regular shape

Gravity – The force between two objects. It pulls things towards the Earth

Hardness – How easy it is to scratch a material. A hard material is difficult to scratch

Heart – The heart pumps blood around the body

Invertebrate – An animal without a backbone

Large intestine – Water from undigested food passes into the body from here

Larva – The young of an animal that hatches from an egg. It is very different from the adult

Lever – A straight rod with a pivot. You can use it to exert a big force over a small distance at one end by exerting a smaller force over a bigger distance at the other end

Light source – An object that makes light

Magnetic force – The force between two magnets, or between a magnet and a magnetic material

Magnetic material – A material that is attracted to a magnet

Medium – A material that sound travels through. A medium can be in the solid, liquid or gas state

Melting – The change of state from solid to liquid

Metamorphosis – When an animal changes completely as it grows

Mixture – A mixture is made up of two or more materials. It is often easy to separate the materials in a mixture

Moon – A natural object that orbits a planet

Muscles – Muscles help animals to move

Not reversible – A change that is not reversible makes new materials. It is difficult – or impossible – to get the starting materials back again

Nutrient – A substance that a plant or animal needs to survive, grow and stay healthy

Oesophagus – Chewed food passes down this tube from the mouth to the stomach

Offspring – The plants or animals that are produced by their parent or parents

Opaque – Light cannot travel through an opaque object

Orbit – The circular (or elliptical) path an object in space takes around another object in space

Pitch – How high or low a sound is

Planet – A big object that orbits a star

Pollination – The transport of pollen from one flower to another

Porous – Water can soak into a porous material

Predator – An animal that eats other animals

Prediction – What you expect to happen in an investigation, based on something you already know or have observed

Prey – An animal that is eaten by other animals

Producer – A living thing that makes its own food. Plants are producers

Proteins – Nutrients needed for growth and repair

Puberty – The stage of life when a child's body matures to become an adult

Pulley – A system of wheels and ropes that make it easier to lift things

Pupa – The third stage in the life cycle of some insects

Reflect – Light is reflected when it bounces off a surface

Relax – When a muscle relaxes, it returns to its original shape

Repel – Push away

Reversible change – A change in which you can get the original materials back. New substances are not made

Sexual reproduction – Making a new living thing by joining pollen with an ovule (in plants) or a sperm with an egg (in animals)

Shadow – An area of darkness on a surface caused by an opaque object blocking out light

Simple machine – A device that changes the direction or size of a force

Skeleton – The structure of bones in a body

Small intestine – Digested food passes into the blood from here

Solar system – The Sun, and the planets and other objects that orbit it

Soluble – A material is soluble if it dissolves in water

Solution – A mixture of a solid with a liquid. You cannot see pieces of solid in a solution

States of matter – The three forms that matter exists in – solid, liquid and gas

Stomach – Digestive juices start to digest food here

Sun – The star at the centre of our solar system

Switch – A component that turns a device on and off

Transparency – A substance is transparent if it lets light through

Variable – Something you can change, measure or keep the same in an investigation

Variation – The differences between animals or plants of the same type

Vertebrate – An animal with a bony skeleton and backbone

Vibrating – An object is vibrating if it is moving backwards and forwards again and again

Vitamins and minerals – Nutrients that keep your body working properly

Volume – The loudness or quietness of a sound

Voltage – The 'push' that makes electricity flow around a circuit

Water cycle – The journey water takes as it circulates from rivers, lakes and seas to the sky and back again

Water resistance – A force that slows things down in water